Philosophical Meta-Reflections on Literary Studies

Philosophical Meta-Reflections on Literary Studies

Why Do Things with Texts, and What to Do with Them?

Jibu Mathew George

ANTHEM PRESS

Anthem Press
An imprint of Wimbledon Publishing Company
www.anthempress.com

This edition first published in UK and USA 2021
by ANTHEM PRESS
75–76 Blackfriars Road, London SE1 8HA, UK
or PO Box 9779, London SW19 7ZG, UK
and
244 Madison Ave #116, New York, NY 10016, USA

First published in the UK and USA by Anthem Press 2019

Copyright © Jibu Mathew George 2021

The author asserts the moral right to be identified as the author of this work.

All rights reserved. Without limiting the rights under copyright reserved above,
no part of this publication may be reproduced, stored or introduced into
a retrieval system, or transmitted, in any form or by any means
(electronic, mechanical, photocopying, recording or otherwise),
without the prior written permission of both the copyright
owner and the above publisher of this book.

British Library Cataloguing-in-Publication Data
A catalogue record for this book is available from the British Library.

Library of Congress Control Number: 2021930107

ISBN-13: 978-1-78527-976-8 (Pbk)
ISBN-10: 1-78527-976-9 (Pbk)

This title is also available as an e-book.

*To the One who engages me on larger questions
and
for Appa, Amma, Celine, Eugene and Juanita*

If you do not feel a generalized intellectual anxiety, if you feel no need to find and make explicit and to evaluate the basic premises of your activities, why the devil philosophize in the first place?

Ernest Gellner

'Iinterpreting' is an intellectual sport […] one that is good for clever people […] who can read and write books about Black sculpture or twelve-tone music but who never get to the heart of a work of art because they stand at the gate fumbling with their hundred keys, blind to the fact that the gate is not really locked.

Hermann Hesse

CONTENTS

Acknowledgements		ix
Introduction		1
1	The Why and Wherefore of Academic Disciplines: The Humanities and the Human World Process	5
	1.1 *The Humanities – An Ugly Duckling among Alma Mater's Pets*	5
	1.2 *The Nature of Knowledge in the Humanities*	7
	1.3 *Obscure or Irrelevant?: The Bogey of 'High Funda'*	9
	1.4 *Implementational and Reflective Intelligence*	11
	1.5 *The Human World Process*	12
	1.6 *An Abstraction Theory of Knowledge*	20
	1.7 *Ontology of the Intangible*	22
	1.8 *Scientific Aspirations of the Humanities*	25
2	If Literature were to Disappear from the Spectrum of Disciplines …	29
	2.1 *Why Do Things with Texts?*	29
	2.2 *Is 'Life' a Humanist Abstraction?*	30
	2.3 *Delicate Epistemes of Literature*	34
	2.4 *Templates of Significance*	43
	2.5 *World-Appetite*	44
	2.6 *Reader-Text Symmetry*	47
3	Beyond for and Against: Tendencies of Contemporary Criticism	53
	3.1 *What to Do with Texts?*	53
	3.2 *The Return of Deductive Reasoning*	54
	3.3 *Facts and Frames*	55
	3.4 *The Enterprise of Ideological Criticism*	57
	3.5 *Constructivism*	61
	3.6 *Ce Qui Arrive (réellement): What Does Deconstruction Actually 'Mean'?*	65
	3.6.1 The Auto-Epiphany of Western Thought	69
	3.6.2 'Put a Pin in That Chap, Will You?': Deconstruction in Critical Practice	70
	3.7 *Why not 'Work' and 'Text'?*	74

	3.8 From Textual Being to Avant-Textual Becoming: A Temporal Ontology for Texts	77
	3.9 The Calculi of Reasoning in Literary Studies	89
4	The Aesthetic and the Political	93
	4.1 The Scandal Called the Aesthetic	93
	4.2 What Is a Classic?	96
	4.3 'Keep the Professors Busy for Centuries'	98
	4.4 A Milestone Approach	101
	4.5 Ever-Changing Domains of Knowledge	106
	4.6 Negotiated Possibilities	108
References		111
Index		119

ACKNOWLEDGEMENTS

In the journey which produced this book, I have accumulated several scholarly and personal debts. I am deeply grateful to everyone with whom I interacted – sometimes in 'virtual space' – in the last four years, since my quotidian reflections began to cross disciplinary boundaries and became self-conscious of domain-specific canons of reasoning.

I am indebted to the reviewers of the manuscript, who provided insightful comments; and Tej P. S. Sood, Megan Greiving, Abi Pandey, Kani and Kyra Droog at Anthem Press, for their support throughout the process of publication.

I am particularly thankful to:

Prof. Christian Tapp, Department of Christian Philosophy, University of Innsbruck, the magnanimous well-wisher whose interventions have helped me see clearly the intersections and divergences of philosophy and literature;

Prof. E. Suresh Kumar, the honourable Vice Chancellor, The English and Foreign Languages University, Hyderabad, for convincing me how important it is to collaborate, and for granting me the time and impetus to focus on research;

Prof. T. Sriraman, an early reader of the manuscript in its original form;

Prof. T. Samson, Dean, School of Literary Studies, The English and Foreign Languages University, Hyderabad, for his insightful observations on post-structuralism and the intellectual antecedents of several contemporary ideas;

Prof. Pramod K. Nayar, Department of English, University of Hyderabad, for his encouragement;

Prof. Udaya Kumar, Centre for English Studies, Jawaharlal Nehru University, New Delhi, whose observations on James Joyce for ever changed my views on doing things with texts;

Dr Mathew John Kokkatt, Department of German, The English and Foreign Languages University, Hyderabad, my constant interlocutor;

Prof. D. Venkat Rao, Department of English Literature, The English and Foreign Languages University, Hyderabad, brief meetings with whom redirect me to matters that matter;

Prof. Syed Sayeed, Department of Aesthetics and Philosophy, The English and Foreign Languages University, Hyderabad, for the immensely fruitful conversations;

Prof. Mahasweta Sengupta, who made available to me her excellent collection of books;

Prof. Gautam Sengupta, whose statements from an analytic philosophy perspective turned my thoughts in a new direction;

Dr Rajiv C. Krishnan, Department of English Literature, The English and Foreign Languages University, Hyderabad, whose sharpest editorial criticism in the past made me an author;

Prof. Arnar Árnason, Department of Anthropology, University of Aberdeen, whose feedback on an earlier article – 'James Joyce and the "Strolling Mort": Significations of Death in *Ulysses*' – I shall cherish;

Dr Rahul Kamble, friend and colleague, the lunchtime conversations with whom have been a great source of encouragement;

Dr Kshema Jose, Department of Training and Development, The English and Foreign Languages University, Hyderabad, whose averment concerning the exclusively 'practical' requirements of knowledge and 'dissection' of texts finds a response in this book;

Eugene and Juanita, who irreversibly changed the coordinates of my existence and have taught me how closely continuous, as opposed to popular pronouncements, the academic and the experiential realms are;

Jeena Elizabeth George, my sister, who took the time to enquire about the progress of my various manuscripts;

Rev. Zachariah Alexander, who provided me forums outside academia to articulate my thoughts and

My students, for being the interlocutors I have desired and needed.

I owe a lot to Prof. Babu Thaliath, Centre for German Studies, Jawaharlal Nehru University; Prof. C. T. Indra, retired Professor and Head, Department of English, University of Madras; Prof. Lee Irwin, Department of Religious Studies, College of Charleston; Prof. Geert Lernout, Department of Literature, University of Antwerp; Prof. Anne C. Fogarty, School of English, Drama and Film, University College Dublin; Prof. Roland Greene, Department of English, Stanford University; Prof. Galin Tihanov, School of Languages, Linguistics and Film, Queen Mary University of London; Prof. Adelina Angusheva-Tihanov, School of Arts, Languages and Culture, The University of Manchester; Prof. Lakshmi Chandra, School of Distance Education, The English and Foreign Languages University, Hyderabad; Prof. T. Nageswara Rao, Department of Indian and World Literatures, The English and Foreign Languages University, Hyderabad; and Prof. Anna Kurian James, Department of English, University of Hyderabad.

ACKNOWLEDGEMENTS

A part of Chapter 3, dealing with deconstruction, has appeared in an earlier version in the collection of essays entitled *Structure and Signs of Play: Derrida/Deconstruction@50* guest edited by Prof. Pramod K. Nayar and published by Padma Prakash for Iris Knowledge Foundation, Mumbai. I am grateful to the editor and the publisher in this endeavour to republish the material in a larger context.

INTRODUCTION

This book takes up key meta-questions in the humanities, with a focus on contemporary literary studies, philosophically examines the nature of knowledge therein and addresses the effervescent question of 'relevance'. Its subtitle is a variation on the title of M. H. Abrams's collection of essays and reviews *Doing Things with Texts* (1989), which in turn echoes J. L. Austin's influential work *How to Do Things with Words* (1955). Effective research and teaching in any discipline depend upon being able to understand its *raison d'être* and the modes of reasoning possible in it. Chapter 1 endeavours to articulate a philosophical rationale for the existence of the humanities with reference to what it calls the human world process. The purpose of theory and philosophy lies in offering a conceptual grasp on the world and a clarification of our implicit assumptions. The chapter argues that knowledge in the humanities is of a different order from that in the sciences and so is its social relevance. Humanistic knowledge has broader subjective and cultural bases and demands articulation of its connections to the 'real' world, to everyday life. The chapter presents a critique of the *minimalist criterion of knowledge*, and enunciates possibilities of cross-fertilization between the academic and the experiential, making a distinction between reflective and implementational intelligence – a distinction reinforced by a fallacy of cognitive ease. Regardless of apprehensions concerning 'grand' concepts, the larger terrain of the humanities is the human world process and the cognitive, cultural, linguistic, interpretive and representational dynamism that endeavours to grapple with the process. The process far exceeds the cognitive, cultural, linguistic, interpretive and representational strategies that seek to capture it. As such, knowledge in the humanities, at least more so than is the case with knowledge of physical objects, is only *an abstracted version* of the process. Further, a characteristic of knowledge in the humanities is that they largely deal with intangible entities, and necessitate an *ontology of the intangible*. The humanities, having had the reputation of a 'soft' discipline, also evince scientific aspirations, as demonstrated by the popularity of impersonal systems and codes in the study of literature and culture.

Chapter 2 introduces a threefold rationale for literary studies – *delicate epistemes, templates of significance* and *world-appetite*. Literature is a discourse which validates, or at least accommodates, *delicate epistemes*. The object of delicate knowledge is something which we are compelled to be apologetic about, in the face of logical fastidiousness, and is not easily amenable to rational demonstration or empirical verification. It is a kind of reality which can resist easy subsumption under ready-made concepts and is vulnerable to the charge of stating the obvious. It is known only through creative, intuitive and sensitive experience. The imperative is to supplement the *hermeneutic of epistemic fastidiousness* (a hermeneutic that 'filters out') with a *hermeneutic of delicate epistemes* (a hermeneutic that 'lets in'). Engaging the post-structuralist position that 'life', an operative word for literature, could be a humanist abstraction, the chapter explains the problem in terms of a hierarchy of concepts – from the abstract macro-concepts at the top to micro-concepts with particular references at the bottom. A second rationale for literature is that it furnishes what one may call *templates of significance*. While delicate epistemes of literature salvage and foreground apparently insignificant, elusive and hard-to-articulate realities, literary templates help organize these amorphous realities into patterns of significance. The third rationale for literature is a *world-appetite*, a proposed supplement to Johann Paul Friedrich Richter's *Weltschmerzen*, 'world-pain' or 'world-weariness'. Human capacity for world-comprehension fails to match up with *world-appetite*. The chapter goes on to argue that response to literary art is a matter of *reader-text symmetry*. With an example from the philosophy of religion, it illustrates that such symmetries and textualities are relevant beyond literary studies.

Chapter 3 philosophically examines the implications of, and assumptions behind, three popular tendencies in contemporary literary criticism – textual deconstruction, ideological criticism and constructivism. Examining the exact relation between theoretical frameworks and the objects of study, the chapter shows how the replication of theoretical assumptions with regard to more and more objects (texts, here) can be a form of deductive reasoning. If theory is a set of concepts that can be used as an explanatory/interpretive framework, are these concepts intrinsic or extrinsic to the object of explanation/interpretation? Behind the decision to 'cathect' a particular idea or theory is *a penchant for embeddedness*, the desire or need to see one's experience as part of a larger framework, phenomenon or ensemble. The chapter posits the possibility of a meta-position with regard to ideological conditioning. To give up such a possibility is to succumb to what may be called *cultural fatalism*. With the concept of the human as an example, the chapter demonstrates that constructivism need not always be emancipatory. Instead, it argues that the validity of conceptual constructivism depends upon the nature of the other discourses upon which constructivist challenges to the concept have a bearing – whether it is a *discourse of rights* or a *discourse of qualification*. Deconstruction reveals a gaping gulf that opens between *world-conceptualization* in language and *world-excess* – an assertion of the latter against a whole self-assured history of the former. Practical criticism involves simultaneous consideration of the object of study both as a work and as a text. In a section pertinently entitled 'From Textual Being to Avant-Textual Becoming', the chapter shows how genetic criticism posits a temporal ontology for texts and outlines the implications thereof. The final section of the chapter clarifies the calculi of reasoning in literary studies – the possibilities offered by analogous reasoning.

Chapter 4 looks at the relation between the aesthetic and the political through non-reductive reasoning. A lot of contemporary criticism seems to collapse the two categories into each other. The chapter takes up the question of what a classic is and argues that the so-called test-of-time criterion is actually a method, not a criterion. Instead, it proposes a milestone approach to defining a classic. It contends that a work needs to be considered significant or insignificant not because it passes or does not pass the test of time, but because it engages substantial political, cultural, social, philosophical and aesthetic questions. The chapter also examines historical changes in the domain of knowledge, which are not merely due to the temporal character of knowledge-advances. Historically, the legitimacy of knowledge depended more on power and ideology than on intrinsic worth. As a result of historical–ideological scrutiny, disciplines have become self-conscious today. The dynamic character of knowledge has enabled several previously excluded social and ethnic groups to have their concerns accepted as legitimate academic subject-matter. The final section of the chapter looks at a paradox of existence – many of its aspects that are contested as ideological and power-driven are also its props and mainstays. A possible response to this paradox is a productively oxymoronic approach of diligent negotiation, by which one can make use of what one is offered as a resource of life while critically understanding its true nature.

Chapter 1

THE WHY AND WHEREFORE OF ACADEMIC DISCIPLINES: THE HUMANITIES AND THE HUMAN WORLD PROCESS

1.1 The Humanities – An Ugly Duckling among Alma Mater's Pets

One principle dominates contemporary deliberations on curriculum planning and development in higher education: 'social relevance'. The one reason given for poor research funding in the humanities is that its results are not immediate. What is not immediate is purportedly irrelevant! At least in Hans Christian Anderson's tale, the ugly duckling eventually reveals itself to be a swan. We are not claiming that the true identity of the humanities will be revealed only in future though this chapter contains a sort of blue print for their expansion. Nor are we saying that we should divert all the funding from stem cell studies and cancer drug research to knowledge generation in the humanities. Ours is not a plea for pre-eminence of the humanities or a plea against any other discipline or set of disciplines, say STEM (science, technology, engineering and mathematics). This is not a plea at all. No discipline needs a defence against any other discipline. As demonstrated with the later discussion of ideological criticism in Chapter 3, polemical or contestational reasoning is a *necessary but insufficient* phase of reasoning in the humanities. But every discipline needs to articulate a rationale for its existence. The title of this section, therefore, is not a summary but a point of departure.

Though in a very different context, some acknowledgements of limitations, or calls for such an acknowledgement, have come from within the humanities. Several years ago, philosopher (or 'post-philosopher') Richard Rorty proposed a modest conversational theory of knowledge. According to him, philosophy was a form of cultured conversation, not an attempted revelation of the truth of the world. Apparently, there is very less at stake here. Rorty was of the view that philosophers should give up the ambition or pretension to describe the world. As the title of his book *Philosophy and the Mirror of Nature* suggests, ideas do not provide a mirror of the way the world is but have consequences. The philosopher is not a 'cultural overseer who knows everyone's common ground' and who offers an explanatory master discourse but an 'informed dilettante' who sees 'relations between various discourses as those strands in a possible conversation' (1990, 316–17). Rorty's was a response to what he called the 'self-obsessed, "in-grown", and "over-philosophized"' character which the humanities had attained in the 1980s. This, according to Rorty, had led to stagnation and the policing of subject areas in universities, whereas his ideal vision of the humanities is one in which they change 'fast enough so that they remain indefinable and unmanageable', which can be brought about through 'good old-fashioned academic freedom' (1999, 129–30). Let us revert to what may be considered an old-fashioned view of the humanities.

It has been more than half a century since J. H. Plumb edited a small volume called *Crisis in the Humanities* (1964). It began with the following sentences: 'Quips from Cicero are uncommon in the engineers' lab; Ahab and Jael rarely provide a parable for biologists; and few hearts swell with pride in Mosley Road Secondary Modern School at the thought of Magna Carta or Waterloo. And how many families sit of a Sunday afternoon listening to father reading *Dombey and Son*?' (1964, 7). That was still a time when 'culture' continued to be viewed as a matter of personal cultivation (true to its Latin etymology), source of inspiration and guidance and, of course, social capital, when 'a tradition of culture, based on the Classics, on Scripture, on History and Literature, bound the governing classes together and projected the image of a gentleman' (7). We hardly find nostalgic dirges of this kind in contemporary writing on the humanities. A strand of thought that runs through Plumb's volume is that the subjects, authors and texts whose loss was lamented then, no longer prepared students for a career in the larger world, with only a few acquiring, or feeling the need for acquiring, the specialized acumen needed to deal with these in a university or college setting. The nature of experience has inevitably changed. Repertoire of the quotidian has changed. Classics are still read for 'imaginative satisfaction' ('Homer sells by millions'; Plumb 1964, 8), but resources for mental and moral formation have also changed in character and availability. So have values. Today, many consciously work to develop the qualities which Arthur Miller's Willy Loman might have admired. Perhaps more important than this historical change (the question is not exactly whether you teach about the past or the present) is the still valid difference between the 'general' student in higher education and the would-be academic 'specialist' – in today's globalized context, that between a would-be content writer for the web or a call-centre executive on the one hand and a wannabe professor on the other.

Do you want to join an accent neutralization course or study Heidegger? Obviously, none can underestimate the value of job-fetching, income-generating 'life-skills'. However, reflections on the other kind of knowledge can yield alternative perspectives.

1.2 The Nature of Knowledge in the Humanities

How knowledge (for the time being, let us lay aside the school of thought which claims that what the humanities generates is not knowledge, in the sense of skill, but understanding) in the humanities matters to society at large is a question which demands an elaborate response. One is often asked rhetorical questions about the relevance of the 'high funda' stuff that is taught under the rubric of theory/philosophy: 'Why can't we lead a simple life?' 'Why do we need Kant and Derrida?' My response to the question is twofold. First, we need concepts to understand and deal with the world. The richer our repertoire of concepts, the more meaningful the world is for us. An example more concrete than one which illustrates Immanuel Kant's 'categories of understanding' would be appropriate here. If one does not have the concept of hands-free phones, walking on an urban street, one might conclude that there are a lot of people who spend time talking to themselves! As we shall see later, the human world – that of institutions, discourses, events, movements, interests, motives and rights – is so complex and elusive that one's search for concepts remains ever-incomplete. The second response pertains to the clarification of assumptions which underlie the way we think, speak and act. In our day-to-day lives we take many things for granted. We socially inherit notions and lead our lives assuming that these are 'eternal verities'. The result is subservience to habit. Something appears good because we have been doing it for a long time. We need 'theory' and 'philosophy' (one can also call it a bit of reflection) to clarify and contest the unconscious assumptions.

A student on my course 'The Holocaust: Paradigms of Thought' once enquired: 'Why did a philosopher like Heidegger *not* intervene to prevent the Holocaust?' If we leave aside for a while Heidegger's membership of the Nazi Party, and the subtle connection of this political affiliation to the complex idea of Being, we may see beneath the question the assumption that philosophers are expected to intervene in crises such as a genocide. It might be a legitimate expectation, but what is of import to us is that this expectation – that ethical initiative *must* follow wisdom and understanding – is assumed as the basis of further debate. To give a more mundane example, there are 'mythologies' (if you are interested in this usage of the word by Roland Barthes) – a structure of assumptions and meanings – that lie behind a student's decision to spend time in the cafeteria than in the classroom (no irony intended).

Knowledge in the humanities is of a different order from that in the sciences. So is its social relevance. This is because the nature of the human world, and of its processes, is radically different from that of the physical world (we shall return to this point shortly). The former is a domain of so many entanglements that it is easy for speculations here to strain into the terrain we have traditionally called 'metaphysics'. Wilhelm Dilthey (1833–1911), German psychologist, historian and hermeneutic philosopher, made a distinction between the methods of natural and physical sciences (*Naturwissenschaften*) and those of the humanities and social sciences (*Geisteswissenschaften*) – *Erklären* (law-governed causal explanation) for the former, and *Verstehen* (interpretive understanding) for the latter. Dilthey's example of *Geisteswissenschaften* (literally, studies of the spirit or mind; but bear in mind that the word *Geist* in German also connotes the true reality of things) was history. Understanding, in Dilthey's 'historical' sense, meant 're-experiencing' (*nachfühlen*) 'alien states of mind' (Ormiston and Schrift 1990, 101) objectified in documents from the past in order to discover the inner feelings and motivations of historical actors. Humanistic knowledge has broader subjective and cultural bases. No wonder Heisenberg's 'uncertainty principle' and Einstein's 'theory of relativity' are hot favourites in the humanities, often tangentially or analogously, and sometimes outlandishly. Further, in the humanities, as postmodernism would have it, a lot of knowledge is not only articulated and circulated in discourse but also created through it – in a repudiation of the traditional 'mirror epistemology'.

The impact of knowledge in the humanities is not as *immediate* as in other fields. This knowledge has less stakes than, say the discovery concerning the retreat of glaciers has. Perhaps, in the long run we shall move towards a qualified generalization which places the sciences in the 'means' column of knowledge and the humanities in the 'ends' column (provided they make use of their innate possibilities). When Parkinson's disease is treated with the psychoactive drug Levodopa, it causes dyskinesia (rapid involuntary movement of the limbs) in the patients. A life scientist discovers that if melatonin, an antioxidant, is prescribed along with the drug, it reduces the progressive nature of this neurodegenerative disorder (Borah and Mohanakumar 2009). The difference between this kind of knowledge and the knowledge in the humanities is manifold. When a life scientist tells us this, we in the humanities are convinced not only that his/her discipline has a greater extra-linguistic grasp over reality than ours can claim. More importantly, knowledge in the humanities demands articulation of its uncanny connections to the 'real' world, to everyday life. Making the connection itself is a higher-order activity. There exist links between Judith Butler's theories of gender and familial prescriptions for the girl child, and between the Foucauldian concept of discourse and contemporary psychiatric practices. These connections are not immediate and obvious. If one were to abide by the immediacy criterion of social relevance, many concepts and fields of study stand in danger of being thrown into the dustbin of intellectual history. In literary studies, only one kind of critical exercise appears to have passed the immediacy-relevance test – ideological criticism. What can we deduce from this? Only when knowledge is perceived as involving power – either to exercise power in/through knowledge, or to contest it – does it draw our attention. Knowledge has to be political in order to be relevant! We know the importance accorded to the humanities (particularly to the field called area studies) during the Cold War period in American universities, and the impetus literary studies has received from postcolonial studies. Indeed we can make intelligent and significant findings in any of the fields and sub-fields or on any concept in socially and politically engaging ways.

1.3 Obscure or Irrelevant?: The Bogey of 'High Funda'

The sociological aspects of the relevance question are more interesting. After a critical theory class which discussed Jean-François Lyotard's *The Postmodern Condition: A Report on Knowledge*, a student asked privately: 'Does this mean anything for the man on the street?' Her legitimate question deserves a response. It is: Isn't it desirable that everyone on the street comes to see the metanarratives that litter everyday life? Isn't it one of the ideals of democratization in higher education, which we have belatedly pursued? The fallacy here is to take the historical denial of higher education to a majority, who has had to struggle to meet basic needs, and their lack of access to complex concepts, as the criterion for the validity of knowledge itself. An aberration cannot be a norm. I consider this *minimalist criterion of knowledge* unconducive to advances in higher education, particularly in the humanities. Honestly, given a choice, would anyone not have preferred an education which equips them to deal with complex concepts? One does require a repertory of concepts and skills to decide the relevance and suitability of knowledge. The social imperative of education is to ensure that everyone has access to the repertory.

One finds Terry Eagleton's rhetorical question 'What does postmodernism mean in Mali or Mayo?' (1996, 72; there must be a postcolonial response to it) an anomaly in his otherwise interesting narrative of literary studies. Consider the following statement of his: 'There is something a little disturbing about this self-indulgent avant-garde hedonism [his reference is to Roland Barthes's post-structuralist criticism] in a world where others lack not only books but food [...] Are there not issues in the world more weighty than codes, signifiers and reading subjects?' (168). For a limited point of comparison, let us recollect one of the common objections to India's nuclear tests in 1998: 'Can a country wherein a vast majority does not have one square meal a day afford to spend on nuclear weapons?' Do the food-security programme and the nuclear weapons programme serve the same purpose? One is not a substitute for the other. Given the scarcity of resources, of course, you need to prioritize. But can you? You decide whether nuclear weapons are necessary or not, on the basis of the security situation, not on the basis of harvests. You can say that one has to satisfy one's hunger before one can think of education. But just as you cannot eat bombs, so you cannot meet the intellectual needs of a society using a full granary.

The link between the academic and the quotidian is not a one-way street either. Conversely, the world outside prepares you for academics. As a matter of fact, every great idea in the history of thought has grown out of everyday reflections. We shall discuss the possible openings for cross-fertilization in Chapter 2, in the section on reader-text symmetry. We know, however, Raymond Williams's brilliant example of such cross-fertilization in a different context. At Cambridge, L. C. Knights claimed in a lecture that 'the word "neighbour" in Shakespeare indicated something that *no* twentieth-century person can understand, because it signified a whole series of obligations and recognitions over and above the mere fact of physical proximity' (Williams 1989, 113; italics as in the source). Williams got up and said that he 'knew perfectly well what "neighbour", in that full sense, means' (114). Williams's growing up in the working-class milieu of twentieth-century Wales with its communitarian life and sense of mutual obligation enabled him to appreciate the meaning of the word.

As for obscurity, there is something more to it than Eagleton's following observation on its being relative to areas of specialization: 'Matthew Arnold and T. S. Eliot read like obscurantist jargon to the person-in-the-street unfamiliar with their critical idiom. One person's specialist discourse is another's ordinary language, as anyone familiar with paediatricians or motor mechanics will testify' (Eagleton 1996, 207). J. R. Sargent, an economist, comments in an informal idiom on the obscurity of the specialist's terminology:

> Steering a course between the total abstainers and the terminology-drunks, the professional amateurs and the furbishers of useless apparatus, the economist *moyen sensuel* must uphold his case to the layman and say: 'I must think precisely. I must therefore invent my own terms as necessary, use abstractions which you find tiresome, and make distinctions which bore you. In short, for the progress of my subject, to you I must be obscure'. (1964, 140)

When enunciated first, every concept is 'neologism' or 'jargon' (e.g., Immanuel Kant's 'categorical imperative' or A. N. Whitehead's 'process metaphysics' or Georg Simmel's 'axiological rotation'). But our concern is not what position the specialist can take but complex concepts being part of a general higher education. The sociology of knowledge aspires to answer the obscurity question as well. As stated above, complex concepts are thought of as elitist by definition, accessible only to those who have had a 'privileged' education. Venturing to tackle complexity, it is assumed, is an indulgence. Are we going to prefer objects and tasks which require less cognitive effort just because complex ones were associated with elite groups in the past and others have not been adequately equipped?

1.4 Implementational and Reflective Intelligence

Over a decade of student-reports, conversations with colleagues and uncanny anecdotes have taught me that knowledge in the humanities has greater ramifications for the future of education, social justice and empowerment of citizens. The thrust of the reports, conversations and anecdotes was the question of relevance. Why study a thinker at all? Why pursue a discipline at all? And 'relevance' is a euphemism for utility. The charge against the humanities is that they do not have immediate utility. Then, what kind of knowledge has this utility and is deemed to be of immediate, practical use? Though this debate is old, the questions that it raises, the distinctions that it makes and the values that underlie both have an urgency in our own time. The utilitarian utopia of knowledge is one which churns out clerks, technicians, call-centre personnel, marketing executives and managerial staff. Learning of preferred accents, fashionable idioms, presentation skills and even a sophisticated body language (the right way to shrug your shoulders!) will land you a job in the higher echelons of the economic hierarchy. Reading Heidegger will not, unless you are on the look out for openings in the philosophy departments of colleges and universities. We can designate the virtue of the former by a neologism – implementational intelligence. It is the virtue that one needs in order to be the human counterpart of a cog in the wheel. The function of the systemic wheel is laid out by its designers. The role of the implementer is merely to implement the design, often as unselfconsciously as possible. A system capable of perpetuating itself is in place. It needs its foot soldiers. They may be paid well even in developing countries though not as well as their counterparts in developed countries are. It is their implementational intelligence which is the favoured primary element in the binary practical/theoretical. The opposite, from the 'practical' perspective, has only an academic/theoretical interest. Perhaps the first thinker to discern a distinction of this kind was Immanuel Kant. To Kant, 'education' was different from 'training', the former focusing on reason, character and moral maxims, and the latter concentrating on skills (1997). Such discernment also underlies the emphasis of Educational Perennialism upon reasoning and wisdom as opposed to facts and technical proficiency.

The distinction between the practical and the reflective is reinforced by what may be termed *the fallacy of cognitive ease*. It goes without saying that the most valid forms of knowledge are not necessarily the simplest ones. Beneath the 'cognitive ease' criterion of knowledge is also the unconscious belief that certain forms of knowledge require higher faculties. This is pertinent because many cultures have for long cultivated the belief that certain forms of knowledge are not meant for everybody. In the Indian context, for instance, we know the historical propaganda to the effect that only some, members of particular communities, had the acumen to imbibe higher knowledge. The absence of internal democracy despite universal franchise and 'affirmative action' owes itself to this historical intellectual inequity, and the assumptions attached thereto. Though not immediately recognized, the assumption even today is that 'mass education' has to be provided on an obligatory basis whereas complex forms of knowledge can be served only to a chosen few. But who will decide who belongs to which category? To condescendingly impart one set of 'skills' to one group of educands (with a future implementational function) and to cultivate another kind of intelligence in a different group would replicate the historical patterns of inequality. This is the 'real' academic elitism, in disguise, which should be subject to scrutiny.

1.5 The Human World Process

Although the spirit of the age (*Zeitgeist*) depends upon who one's interlocutors are, if one were to point out the single great characteristic of our times, one could say that it is a ubiquitous blur – a relinquishing of what may be called a 'will to reality'. One of the several caveats for making a statement about anything these days is that the object, event or phenomenon about which the statement is made, is unknowable, at least in its entirety, or in a 'hypothetical' pure form. Take, for instance, the contemporary philosophy of history. The postmodern philosophy of history, represented by Hayden White (1928–2018), seems to have found the enterprise of the nineteenth-century German historian Leopold von Ranke not only impossible but also undesirable. Ranke believed that the historian's job was to reconstruct the past 'as it actually was' (*wie es eigentlich gewesen war*). History is always written from the perspective of the present and serves purposes of the present. Hayden White in his *Metahistory: The Historical Imagination in Nineteenth-Century Europe* (1973) sets out to demonstrate that historical narratives are neither simple representations of a sequence of events nor the revelation of a design inherent in them. Instead, White analyzes historical narratives as shaped by the imposition on events of cultural patterns similar to narratological concepts such as plot and character type. If one examines White's narrativization thesis a bit rigorously, one may find two histories – history as discourse and history as referent. Further, there are three questions (postmodern historiography has conflated them) that intervene in the gap between the putative referent and the available narrative discourse: (1) Did the event (the referent) actually occur?[1] (a yes-or-no question); (2) What is the nature of the event?; (3) In weaving a coherent narrative, what elements of the referent were included and excluded? The three questions are not confined to watertight compartments but are mutually trespassable. What is true of historical accounts is also true of media stories, which is in a sense everyday historiography.

Though this is not the fashionable position to take in the contemporary theoretical climate, I will stick my neck out and say that the humanities are about the *human world process*. Though the human world process is far more dynamic than the processes of the physical world, it has been sometimes considered analogous to the physical. When Auguste Comte first proposed the study of social facts, the alternative name he gave Sociology was *Social Physics*, and 'Comte's first critic and expositor in the [British] islands, Sir David Brewster, a Scots physicist, accepted the term *social physics* in 1838 without demur in the midst of his hostile account of Comte's *Cours de philosophie positive*' (MacRae 1964, 124).

Let me present the human world process in a microcosm, in an immediate version. When I return from work at the university in the evening, I perceive the city streaming (I know it only on the surface, but no doubt there is a process on, with all its charm and cussedness): people returning from work, or going to work in night shifts in factories or call centres; construction of the metropolitan railway network; carpooling companies contacting their prospective clients; relatives, friends and acquaintances meeting up after a long time; petty squabbles; clandestine flirtations; dining and dancing; chatting and cheating. The process is proliferent, unwieldy, elusive, multistranded and entangled. You can make anything of this process. You can theorize the urban anonymity of everyday life in the modern world (or the modernist alienation), look for Charles Baudelaire's and Walter Benjamin's *flâneur* (the gentleman stroller of the streets), or for Michel de Certeau's practice of everyday life (counter-practices which subvert pre-imposed designs through alternative use of what is given). The human world process also includes what we think, or are made to think. Emotions, motives, interests and moods, ethos and mores, cultural conditioning and ideological influences, inherited narratives and world views, propaganda and persuasion are all part of the process. It is not that you have your narrative of the world, or a world view, and I have mine. Our narratives, ideologies, world views and cognitions are the engine for the forward movement of the human world process. The way we think takes the process forward.

Now let me give an example of the process in its macrocosmic, unimmediate version. It may not be an easily accepted one for the postmodern scepticism towards grand narratives, but here it is. According to Oswald Spengler (1880–1936), the unit of human history is not an 'epoch' (such as ancient, medieval and modern),[2] but a 'culture'. Drawing upon Goethe's work *Metamorphosis of Plants* (1790), Spengler proposes in *The Decline of the West* (1895–1920) that cultures are like organisms; they grow, mature, decay and ultimately die. Their 'destiny' and 'direction' are determined by an 'inward necessity' (1926, 31), but the culture is largely unconscious of it. World history is the biography of their organic evolution, actualizing the culture's 'soul', or 'becoming', whose living logic is unamenable to rigid cause-and-effect analysis. A culture is the sum total of its inner possibilities and actualities. As the botanist, with knowledge of a plant's genus and species, can predict its future, so a philosopher of history can predict the future of the cultural organism.

In contradistinction to the then-popular European narrative of unstoppable linear progress, Spengler claims that cultures, like organisms, have only a limited life span. It is this finite character of historical existence which distinguishes Spengler's thesis from even other critiques of the European 'progress' narrative. The decline of a culture is the completion of an inwardly necessary evolution. Like a plant, a culture also sprouts, blooms, ripens, wilts and dies. Its trajectory is not of endless fruition but of temporally limited growth, and inevitable, irrevocable end. The implication is that those who have witnessed blooming and ripening must also witness wilting and dying. Each culture has an approximate life span of one thousand years, and passes through periods of youth, maturity and age.

Spengler discusses the life cycle of a culture in terms of seasons, as Northrop Frye (1957) analyses literary genres – spring, summer, autumn and winter. The spring phase witnesses the origin of a culture's principles. Western culture experienced this phase from 1000 to 1500 AD. It was heroic, feudal and deeply religious. During the summer phase (1500–1800 AD), the principles of the culture develop fully. In the Western world this phase featured dynastic monarchy, refinement of manners, struggle between rational and mystical modes of thought, leading to magnificent creativity, wars fought in accordance with traditions of honour, and equal prominence for the city and the countryside. The autumn phase (1800–2000 AD) is called the Age of Contending States, and is marked by the rise of world-cities, cultural impoverishment of the countryside,[3] rise of democracy, depopulation, dissolution of certainties of knowledge into relationships (Spengler's example is Nietzsche's 'transvaluation of values'), transformation of philosophical systems to meet practical needs (what is called *Gelegenheitsdenken* – literally, opportunity-thinking; e.g., utilitarianism) and decline in artistic creativity. The final stage of culture is called 'civilization',[4] when it loses its vitality, its sustaining principles breakdown and it sinks into sterility and decline. This is the winter phase. For the Western culture, this phase falls in the first few centuries of the new millennium. It is characterized by Caesarism (a kind of government devoid of any political form, whose authority has no constitutional foundations), globally homogenized life practices, subordination of economics to politics, concentration of wealth in the hands of a few, private politics and private wars, a plutocratic and manipulative press, revolt of uprooted megalopolitan masses and a formulaic art of spectacle.

Spengler recognizes eight 'High Cultures' or *Hochkulturen*, namely Babylonian, Egyptian, Chinese, Indian, Mexican (Mayan/Aztec), Classical, Magian and Faustian, but devotes most of his discussion to the last three. Classical or Apollonian culture is his term for cultures of Mediterranean antiquity – the Graeco-Roman. Magian culture consists of Jewish, Aramaic, Nestorian, Zoroastrian-Persian and Islamic elements, Islam being 'the final expression' of the Magian soul. Modern Western or 'Euro-American' culture is what he calls 'Faustian'.

The soul of a culture expresses itself in political systems, structures and styles of government, social forms, laws, manners and morals, religion, art, science, mathematics, economy and, above all, its world view (*Weltanschauung*). Spengler indicates the holistic cultural significance of myriad phenomena repeatedly using the famous lines from Goethe's *Faust II*: *Alles vergängliche ist nur ein Gleichnis* (All that passes is a symbol). Art has a special place in Spengler's schema. It is the 'prime phenomenon' of the Faustian culture; its destiny is decipherable in art. It is Goethe whom Spengler cites as an intellectual precursor, and from whose magnum opus he borrows the Faust-figure to be an embodiment of modern Western culture – not Hegel, with whose philosophy of history Spengler's own work has the closest resemblance. The Faust figure, originally taken from the Teutonic legend, also Goethe's protagonist, is a proud, creative and tragic figure, who strives after unlimited power and knowledge – the unattainable. So does the Western culture yearn for the infinite and the distant. Thomas Mann, in his novel *Docktor Faustus* (1947), was to rewrite the Faust legend again after World War II in an allegory of the German nation which had sold its soul to the devil – here, the Nazi regime.

Every culture has an Ur-symbol or prime symbol, chosen at the time of its awakening, through which it apprehends the world, and endeavours to overcome the fear of death. The symbols of a culture are an expression of its inner world-feeling, and are meaningful to its members alone; they are incomprehensible to outsiders, who do not share its world-feeling. The prime symbol of the ancient Egyptian culture was 'the way' (even beyond life in this world), actualized in the pyramid, the tomb temple and the sarcophagus. The Magian soul expresses itself in the cavern idea, symbolized by the central dome of a mosque. The prime symbol of the Classical/Apollonian culture is the definite, separate body, whose beauty was appreciated, but which conception, according to Spengler, accounted for the 'limited' world view of the Greeks and 'rigid' forms in every sphere of life. For example, the Greek *polis* is the smallest conceivable political unit, and everything outside was considered hostile, its public life limited to the *agora*. In principle, the *polis* was inextensible, though its population could increase. Classical mathematics, with fixed definite shapes and finite integers, and no irrational numbers or variables, evinces a fear of the immeasurable and the infinite. Classical time absorbed all past in the present, which, according to Spengler, led to an 'ahistorical' existence (Spengler 1926, 147). All past is equally distant, and Alexander of Macedonia could declare himself the son of a god, Zeus, thus making no distinction between mythical and historical temporalities. For Spengler, Immanuel Kant, in positing time as a category, and depriving it of directionality, was Classical in his world-feeling. Spengler's corrective to Kant is that space is a form of the perceived, and time that of perception.

The prime symbol of the Faustian culture is 'pure and limitless space' (Spengler 1926, 183), or infinite space. While the Classical symbol of finite bodies is one of the already become, the Faustian symbol of boundless space symbolizes infinite becoming. The Faustian temporal sense is futuristic. Historically, the Faustian spirit of infinite striving expressed itself in:

1. the longing for the infinite, or a transcendent God-feeling, expressed in Western monotheism;[5]
2. the attempt to understand the inscrutable and the incalculable by positing concepts such as grace;
3. the soaring gothic spires which defy gravity and Euclidean geometry;
4. Leibniz's infinitesimal calculus in mathematics;
5. geographical exploration, migration, imperial expansion, conquest and empire;
6. inventions and discoveries;
7. the ambitiously executed idea of perpetual motion of machines;
8. railways, shipping and aviation;
9. monetary proliferation using credit banking system, which opened up continents and released Faustian financial energies across them;
10. globalization;
11. the legends of the grail quest, and the *Sturm and Drang* movement;

12. the vast surfaces, depths and distances in painting, as in the remote horizon and limitless range of Caspar David Friedrich's *Wanderer above the Sea of Fog* (1818);
13. the notion of evolving personality in the Western tragedy as opposed to the static and type characters in Attic tragedy;[6]
14. the 'beyond-ness' of the swelling and transcending polyphony;[7]
15. crusades and proselytization enterprises;[8]
16. the unrelenting, unabatable will to power which added to the virulence of the struggle between empire and papacy (the great Faustian dissidence);
17. realization of individual possibilities through a personal culture, as evident in the writing of autobiographies and memoirs;[9]
18. the invention of printing, which connotes distance, duration and dissemination;[10]
19. the spirit of enquiry and nature research extending from the Jesuits through Francis Bacon to Charles Darwin, and collection of countless facts, as evident in Denis Diderot's *L'Encyclopaedie*;
20. the Romantic wistfulness concerning ruins and the distant past;
21. the moral desire for world-improvement[11] and the resultant intolerance, as illustrated by a long period of persecution from the Inquisition and the burning of heretics at the stake to the burning of books (*Bücherverbrennung*) under the Nazi rule and
22. the fiction and dream of resurrecting Imperium Romanum, which extended to the world wars of the twentieth century.

However, like the protagonist of Goethe's *Faust II*, Western culture is in its phase of decay and dying – its winter phase. Spengler uses the word 'decline' in the title to mean a twilight phase[12] of Western culture in consummation or fulfilment of a destiny (*Vollendung*) rather than a catastrophic occurrence. Finally, Faust's energies are exhausted, his ingenuity is used up. To understand the significance of Spengler's contrastive comparisons, we have to consider a certain intertextual influence upon *The Decline of the West*. Spengler was inspired to undertake a civilizational study by Otto Seeck's work *Geschichte des Untergangs der Antiken Welt* (*The Decline of Antiquity*), a social-Darwinist study. In Seeck's social-Darwinist narrative, the weak fall by the wayside in the march of cultures. Herein lies the contrast and its ennobling implications. The Classical world stagnated and declined due to the tyranny of a limited world view; the Faustian universe is declining as a result of restless striving. The contrast is between stasis and striving. The Classical has rusted; the Faustian is worn out through use. The Apollonian culture is marked by the stiff, the rigid, the tendency to hold back and the hesitation to venture forth. The Faustian has overstepped bounds, has ventured forth, taken the deep plunge. Faust's energies are *spent* in tireless and endless striving after limitless power, knowledge and life, in an unreserved expression of inward possibilities. The Classical culture perished because its world view was static, 'not fit enough'; the Faustian culture is dying because Faust's energies are spent in executing his dynamic, overreaching world view. There has been no standing still or turning back in this willed, productive movement. Faustian passion changed the face of the earth. But passion is both enthusiasm and suffering. For his unlimited ambition Faust pays with catastrophe and trauma – the recipe of tragic grandeur. It was not an easy barter but a costly deal. And the fault 'is not in our stars', but in our prime symbols, the world-feeling of our cultures.

How does one make sense of a process which is as long-temporal, spatially proliferent and dispersed in multiple phenomena as the above? It requires models (calling it a process itself indicates the use of a model), generalizations, speculations, interpretations, representative strategies and, above all, use of metaphors (in Spengler's case the controlling figural metaphor of Faust) – all these are attempts to put our finger on the elusive and intriguing process. Indeed the world process is complex, multistranded, proliferent and unwieldy, and it has been tempting to explain it in terms of a single principle, concept or trope. For example, Friedrich Hegel thought of it as the unfolding or outworking of the Absolute spirit; Arthur Schopenhauer explained it in terms of Will (all striving). The Buddha had four principles – the Four Noble Truths: All earthly life is full of sorrow; Desire or craving is the source of sorrow; Sorrow can be averted by giving up craving; and One can give up craving by following the Noble Eight Fold Path (*Āryāṣṭāṅgamārga*) – Right Belief, Right Aim, Right Speech, Right Effort, Right Living, Right Intention, Right Attention and Right Meditation.

Why this reductionism? Social psychologists Susan T. Fiske and Shelley E. Taylor have proposed that the human mind is a 'cognitive miser'. The idea of the mind as a cognitive miser is one of the basic premises of social cognition. The mind looks for the simplest way to negotiate the social world. According to the cognitive miser theory of Fiske and Taylor, the human mind endeavours to understand people and events with the least investment of psychic energy. Being parsimonious in the expenditure of energy, it endeavours to negotiate the world with the least cognitive effort.[13] In its larger attempts to understand the world too, it is economical with the use of cognitive energies.

The earliest of the cognitively economical single concepts/tropes was provided by religion – supernatural agents who regulated the process. Of course, this included processes of both the natural and the human world. Monotheism posits an omniscient, omnipresent and omnipotent God who regulates the process. Polytheism, by definition, multiplies divine entities according to the way in which phenomena, functions and the cosmos itself are divided. The human tropology for the world process encompasses notions of an impersonal order, such as Egyptian *ma'at*; Greek *arché* (its antithesis being *anankē*, errancy and irrationality), *moira* (fate, to which even gods are subject) and *logos* (in the sense of governing reason and organizing principle); Hindu *rta* and the law of *karma* (self-contained causality or fate); Buddhist *samsara* (mechanistic eternal world order) and *nidanas* (a concatenation of cause and effect); and Chinese *dao* (active practice of the order of nature). The tropology extends to modern concepts as diverse as Hegel's Absolute Spirit, whose 'outworking' is the progress of both consciousness and human history; Schopenhauer's Will; Bergson's *élan vital* (vital impetus); and Spengler's inner historical directionality of cultures, albeit with limited explanatory ambitions. These metaphysical and quasi-metaphysical concepts are cognitively economical 'single-entity-tropes' that help apprehend the complex, multistranded and unwieldy world process, and continuous with the tropological gamut of religion. Western attempts at understanding the world process have extended from naturalistic, metaphysical and supernatural conceptions – religious ideas and their philosophical analogues – of the process from the Presocratics (the *physikoi* as opposed to the *theologoi*, in Aristotle's terminology) through exponents of 'fundamental principles', as well as personal and impersonal, theistic and pantheistic orders, down to the self-reflexive turn to the human subject, mental principles (à la Kant) and cultural, linguistic and representational schemata as the ground of world-theorization.

What triggered transitions from a religious to secular world view was a three-fold change in the understanding of the world process. These transitional factors include:

1. 'complexification' (a philosophical concept which has larger implications than the sociological concept of 'differentiation') of the world process with the emergence of several domains – politics, economy, bureaucracy, art, ethics, science and so on – each with its own autonomous, specialized logic, from the age-old obsession with a single explanatory principle or entity, accompanied by a retrospective realization that the latter was a unifying name for many logics;
2. reconceptualization of the world process as not following a fixed trajectory but amenable to human agential alteration, aided by the instrumental efficacy of science and technology; and
3. perceived evidence of an *impersonal logic in a significant analogous system* (e.g., the influence of the impersonal social organization of the *polis* upon Presocratic materialists; Tarnas 2010, 17).

For those who are interested in such a long-historical intellectual trajectory of Western world-theorizing endeavours, a key work is Richard Tarnas's

The Passion of the Western Mind: Understanding the Ideas that have Shaped Our World View (2010).

1.6 An Abstraction Theory of Knowledge

The larger terrain of the humanities is the human world process and the cognitive, cultural, linguistic, interpretive and representational dynamism that endeavours to grapple with the process. Pursuit of any discipline that falls under the rubric of the humanities requires some understanding of how the human world works. What is of further import to us here is that the human world process far exceeds the cognitive, cultural, linguistic, interpretive and representational strategies that seek to capture it. As such knowledge in the humanities, at least more so than is the case with knowledge of physical objects, is only *an abstracted version* of the process. This abstract is passed on and made the basis of further enquiries. It is therefore imperative to be both self-reflexive about the epistemic endeavours and, more importantly, to change the terms of enquiry, if possible, periodically. We are not claiming that if we do this, we shall be able to unravel the process in its entirety – lay down its directions in a map rid of epistemic crinkles. But since the human world process is interconnected, if we re-examine the fundamentals of any human phenomenon, a whole series of phenomena, understandings and histories can change in character. The compulsion to abstract is perhaps true of all human situations. For instance, in a communication, involving the sender, the message, the medium and the receiver, the receiver abstracts only a part of the ensemble of things involved: the message, its linguistic, cultural and psychological nuances, the context and background factors pertaining to the sender and the receiver.

Why do we say that only an abstracted version of the process is available? We say so for several reasons. First, the human world process has, as it were, several strands. The intricacies of each strand of the process are beyond generalizations concerning the process as a whole. These strands – political, economic, social, cultural, psychological and so on – are isolated and parcelled out into concerns of separate disciplines and respective disciplinary terrains. For example, supply and demand, boom and bust, debt financing, speculative capital ('hot money') inflows, and cycles of income, saving, investment, production and employment form its economic strand. Some of these disciplines are designated as social sciences rather than humanities. Philosophy, which apparently has the aura of a meta-humanistic discipline that looks into the process as a whole and attempts to understand it, has diversified into studies of the micro-logic of parts. Hence, we have a philosophy of almost everything: a philosophy of walking, a philosophy of cooking, a philosophy of boredom and what not. Second, humans, both subjects and actants in this process, for pragmatic reasons, are compelled to act on abstracted versions. We endeavour to know only as much as we need to act.

Third, the human world process has micro-logics which macro-generalizations cannot account for. Take, for example, the received idea of the middle ages as a paradigmatic age of faith. But how tenable is this inherited idea? In Chapter 7 of my book *The Ontology of Gods: An Account of Enchantment, Disenchantment, and Re-Enchantment* (2017), I attempt to re-imagine the medieval *Lebenswelt*, that is, reality as actually (often unconsciously) organized and experienced by an individual subject. The common believer prayed to God during the Black Death to spare his son, but the latter died. He prayed for adequate food to feed his family, but had to starve (it is said that some of the so-called visions experienced by people were actually hallucinations produced by extreme starvation, which were a common medieval phenomenon). He asked for a reasonably satisfactory harvest, but it failed. At a time of frequent wars, civil wars, feuds and vendettas, his wife prayed for the safe return of their son, but the young man was killed in ambush. Miracles did not happen; laws, natural and social, inflexibly prevailed. The world process ran its course. There was so little evidence of any extraneous intervention that even in the so-called age of faith, it must have been difficult to sustain faith. It must have been particularly difficult in the medieval epoch *because* it was an age of faith, which emphatically professed a comprehensive divine overview of human destiny. The realization that the given would prevail, or the postulated (divine) forces of reversal of the status quo were indifferent is all the more shocking in an age of faith. How does one deal with this conflict between the all-encompassing religious system and actual experience? This must have been at least as much the source of an enormous cognitive dissonance in the religious subject then as it is today. Faced with experiential non-fulfilment of the religious narrative, the subject has three choices. One, she/he might endeavour to make sense of what happens, or does not happen, within the received schema. Religion is capable of an explanatory adjustment when experience does not match its narrative, and can rationalize such non-fulfilment.[14] Two, the believer might simply cease to believe in God. Atheism based on experience, rather than on intellectual reasoning, is a sign of desperation at the absence of divine intervention. Help does not come, explanation does not come. Traditional narratives of the age of faith take the first of the three possibilities for granted, and rarely, the second. But there is also a third option: A change in the idea of God. God or no-God is not the only option; the alternative is God-as-this versus God-as-that, or God in full control versus God as a nominal presiding or originating force, or even God as a symbol of concerns. Whether this possibility actually materialized or not is a matter of research in *histoire des mentalités* ('history of consciousness').

1.7 Ontology of the Intangible

What is the nature of the human world process? Here I would like to introduce a concept called *the ontology of the intangible*.[15] One of the characteristics, or rather pitfalls, of knowledge in the humanities is that they largely deal with intangible entities – events, ideas, world views, transitions thereof and so on. A further problem is: what kind of reasoning is possible with the intangibles? On what basis can one argue that revolutionary art offers a safety valve permitted by oppressive societies in lieu of actual social change? On what basis can Terry Eagleton, in *The Ideology of the Aesthetic* (1990), construct his quasi-philosophical allegory surrounding the sensuous internalization of historical ideologies/world views and contradictions thereof in the category of the aesthetic? One may object that this is also true of mathematics. But numbers and algebraic expressions are intangible in a way which is different from say, something like an event. Mathematical models can claim a higher degree of equivalence with entities that are there in the world.

What is an event? What we call an event might consist of several constitutive micro-events. When we name historical events, or movements, we name them as macro-events comprising several related micro-events, which can be categorized under one label (e.g., the Renaissance, World War II, and the counterculture of the 1960s). It may be argued that there is no such entity as an event, and the event is merely a concept. This is said primarily because an event is *inextricable*. What is designated as an 'event' emanates in one or many of the precursor events and might extend indistinguishably into the following ones. Alignments of causes and effects never end, and links proliferate both temporally and spatially. Further, an event is a composite entity in another sense – it consists of occurrences, persons, things and states of affairs. The second and third are, of course, tangible. The reality of the event lies in its endless entanglements, and includes the motives and intentions of the actants, the experience and response of those who are acted upon and the significant discourses which are part of the build-up to the putative climax or event-series.

It is the intangible component, which is extra-sensory, and more often than not extra-empirical, which requires interpretation. One of the tasks of philosophy is to decipher the intangible, and more importantly, self-reflexively articulate the methods, possibilities and limitations of this decipherment. Let me cite an example from my studies in the philosophy of the other in relation to extreme experience (George 2010). Extreme experiences are both a test case for ideas and a pretext for their emergence. Experiences such as that of war, of torture, of terminal illness, of other forms of encounter with death, of prolonged imprisonment and of chronic isolation, to name a few, mostly from Judith Herman's *Trauma and Recovery* (1992), are at once overwhelming and delicate – so overwhelming as to trigger shifts in paradigms of understanding and so delicate as to render rigorous frameworks unsuitable. In my article entitled 'Further Explorations in the Philosophy of the Other in Relation to Extreme Experience' (2010), written on the tenth anniversary of the Abu Ghraib prison abuse, I argue that contrary to a lot that is claimed concerning the subject and the object in common parlance, ill treatment, including torture, of another human being is not a case of objectification. In any case, torture is not treating people like objects. Objects are not sentient, and there is no point in torturing objects, unless objects represent something else, for example, an object that is dear to the victim. Though torture crushes the subjectivity of the other, strictly speaking, this is not objectification. We objectify people when we choose not to factor in their responses, or when we behave as if they are not present. In the dialectic of the perpetrator and the victim, responses of the other do matter. The dialectic is marked by a neurotic pursuit of another's subjectivity, a pathological sub-category of what Chapter 2 of this book calls *world-appetite*. In more specific terms, it is a struggle to engage another's subjectivity on one's own terms, 'to teach the other a lesson'. This hypothesis is amply borne out by the details of the way in which the Final Solution to the Jewish Question (*Die Endlösung der Judenfrage*) was implemented. The Schutzstaffel (SS) deliberately chose the days of Jewish festivals as occasions to initiate torture exercises and forced transportation from the ghettoes. The guards asked rabbis to wipe the floor with Torah scrolls. Such symbolic engagements of another's subjectivity do elicit responses. In a singular act of resistance against transportation of Jews, the Jewish Combat Organization launched the near-suicidal Warsaw ghetto uprising on 19 April 1943, the day of *Pesach* (the Passover, symbolizing liberation and commemorating the emancipation from captivity in Egypt).

To slip into the autobiographical, a few years ago, I was exploring the relation between extreme experience and creativity – the connection between unbearable experience – war, genocide and natural disasters, on the one hand, and path-breaking discoveries, paradigm shifts in thought and even experimental art, on the other. I tried two existing explanations. One is the theory of sublimation – channelization of anger and resentment into productive endeavours. According to Carl Gustav Jung, who articulated it in a deliberately anti-Freudian sense, 'Sublimation is part of the royal art where the true gold is made' (Jung 1974, 171). The second explanation is that it is precisely the kind of preceding experience that the consequent achievement requires for its raw material. Viktor Frankl's psychotherapeutic method 'Logotherapy' (based on the 'will to meaning' even in the most harrowing circumstances, as the source of survival) needs for its emergence the experience of the concentration camp. Drawing a similar connection between preceding experience and future praxis, Jung wrote a few days before his death: 'Only the wounded physician can hope to heal'. My supplementary explanation was that the inability of available 'external forms', be it modalities of interpersonal relationships, limitations of language, or existing models of thought or forms of art, to capture the overwhelming intensity, precise nature and the true extent of extreme experience compels the experiencing subjects to break these forms or paradigms, and develop radical alternatives. But I have revised my formulation since then. When experience is overwhelming the human psyche salvages the most delicate and the most vulnerable aspects of reality which it considers valuable. And the capacity to do this increases involuntarily and exponentially. This is also one of the ways in which literary imagination deals with traumatic historical experiences.

Students of literature often ask why writers of traumatic experiences have to take recourse to fictional narratives. The examples they have in mind include Elie Wiesel's *Night Trilogy* and African American novels. Why couldn't those who experienced misery and near-annihilation write a memoir or a survivor testimony? Indeed the possibilities provided by narrative – that is, possibilities of deducing and creating alternative meanings and implications from the same event – have furnished victims of extreme experiences with opportunities to come out of their traumatic labyrinth. As the reappearance of Sethe's child in Toni Morrison's *Beloved* (1987) shows, one cannot wish away the past; it has to be incorporated in a meaning-giving (narrative) framework. We all live by narratives. We can go to bed contented if we can 'emplot' the myriadness of the day into a meaningful and satisfying narrative. Critical emphasis on narratives, representations and discourses also enables us to contest underlying, taken-for-granted assumptions. But we may ask a pertinent question: Does this emphasis, in any way, do injustice to the original experience, the referent? Is there anything about the event itself which militates against prevalent representational, narrative and discursive paradigms – which are often evaluated more for their rhetorical efficacy than for their correspondence to the original experience? When it comes to extreme experiences, bartering 'essences' for heuristic, workable, flexible and contestable constructs is an inadequate compensation for the tantalizing inability to develop a full-fledged ontology of the event or experience in question. In other words, narrative is inevitable but inadequate.

Where else can you find a home for enquiries of the above-mentioned kind except in a discipline (or disciplinary spectrum) which can deal with intangible realities? In the next chapter, we will examine how literature fits into this schema of the human world process.

1.8 Scientistic Aspirations of the Humanities

Regardless of what their practitioners claim, the humanities have had the reputation of being a 'soft discipline'. As for literary studies, among the sceptics of the field, there is a view abroad that in its competition for academic space with the sciences (including the social sciences) on what could hardly be characterized as a 'level playing field', teachers of literature gave up the old school ways of doing literature and took up theory, which not only gave them the aura of interdisciplinary erudition, but, more importantly, a semblance of meeting the requirements of 'hard science'. In any case, certain tendencies in the humanities betray their anxieties of being a sub-discipline – *an ugly duckling among alma mater's pets*. In the humanities in general, and in literary studies in particular, we increasingly notice a tendency to deny agency and to examine dynamic human reality in terms of impersonal systems and codes. Ferdinand de Saussure's theory of language is an early example. One may endeavour to explain this tendency as part of the (unconscious?) scientistic aspirations of the humanities (conversely, the sciences might have humanistic aspirations), embedded in the anxieties of the discipline. Consider Terry Eagleton's summary of Formalism, which typifies the tendency:

> The literary work was neither a vehicle for ideas, a reflection of social reality nor the incarnation of some transcendental truth: it was a material fact, whose functioning could be analysed rather as one could examine *a machine* [emphasis added]. It was made of words, not of objects or feelings, and it was a mistake to see it as the expression of an author's mind. Pushkin's *Eugene Onegin,* Osip Brik once airily remarked, would have been written even if Pushkin had not lived. (1996, 2–3)

The 'things-work-on-their-own' bandwagon has been on the move for quite a few centuries of intellectual history across disciplines – religious studies, linguistics, semiology, anthropology, literary criticism and cultural theory. Probably this was an off-shoot of deism[16] and the 'Disenchantment of the World' (Max Weber's *Entzauberung der Welt*).[17] In fact, the tendency has been prevalent alongside its opposite in many epochs of history. The world emerged and goes on, on its own; there is no prime mover. Language works on its own; there is no intention. We do not speak language; language speaks us. The text creates meanings on its own; authorial intention is irrelevant (According to William K. Wimsatt and Monroe C. Beardsley, it is neither available nor desirable!). Discourse creates subjects; the question of subjectivity does not arise. Everything works on its own. Literary critics became eager to deny the human dynamics underlying most phenomena. With this end in view, literary criticism borrowed avidly from other disciplines, linguistics (Ferdinand de Saussure) and anthropology (Claude Lévi-Strauss) in particular. Choice, intention and agency were abandoned. Probably, this was the result of a disappointment with the soft, effeminate character, or image, of the discipline. In the form of structuralism, criticism began to be 'concerned with structures, and more particularly with examining the general laws by which they work' (Eagleton 1996, 82). Poems, myths and other narratives came to be seen as structures. Food, clothing, kinship, language, cosmos and narrative were systems of signs. The humanities abandoned the human element: 'The mind which does all this thinking is not that of the individual subject: myths think themselves through people, rather than vice versa. They have no origin in a particular consciousness, and no particular end in view' (Eagleton 1996, 90). As far as the discipline's existential crisis was concerned, ideological criticism absolutely fitted the bill (we have a separate section in Chapter 3 on ideological criticism). Structural Marxism, which curiously combined the mechanistic logic with political engagement, also continued the legacy of de Saussure and Lévi-Strauss:

> As far as a science of human societies goes, [...] individuals can be studied simply as the functions, or effects, of this or that social structure – as occupying a place in a mode of production, as a member of a specific social class, and so on. But this of course is not at all the way we actually experience ourselves. We tend to see ourselves rather as free, unified, autonomous, selfgenerating individuals; and unless we did so we would be incapable of playing our parts in social life. For [Louis] Althusser, what allows us to experience ourselves in this way is ideology. (Eagleton 1996, 149)

The latest entrant to the things-work-on-their-own network is the post-structuralist theory of textuality. 'To write' is an intransitive verb. It has neither an object nor a subject (the author is dead).

Notes

1. The problem with considering an event as a referent will be clear when we discuss the ontology of the intangible, which characterizes most of the human world process.
2. Spengler has in mind Jacob Burckhardt's construction of the Renaissance as an epoch.

3   The low status accorded to the countryside is evident in the use of the word 'rusticate'. The Latin participle 'rusticat' means 'having lived in the country'.
4   Note that Spengler differs from Fernand Braudel in the use of the terms 'culture' and 'civilization'. For Braudel, civilization denotes the material basis, whereas culture is the phase of a civilization where higher feats are possible. Braudel belonged to the Annales School of history. Having lived through the two world wars and the political upheavals in France, the Annales School of historians were deeply uncomfortable with the ruptures and discontinuities that traditional historians saw as characterizing history. They believed that beneath the ruptures and discontinuities, a day-to-day life of relative stability and inertia could be discovered. At this micro-level of history, human life is determined not by short-term factors such as the whims and fancies of political leadership but long-term ones such as geography, climate and demography. Beside the latter, the so-called events and upheavals in institutions are of little significance. Braudel demonstrated the operation of such a micro-history in his work *The Mediterranean and the Mediterranean World in the Age of Philip II* (1927–49). He reconstructs the apparently ephemeral lives of slaves, serfs, peasants and the urban poor in terms of their food, clothing, social customs and mentalities, and suggests that these people are the real makers of civilization. For Braudel, history operates at various levels and is subject to various temporalities. He calls the first temporal level the *longue durée* (longer duration) (1980, 208). This is geographical time, in which man interacts with his environment for survival (*histoire structurale*, or structural history). Changes in geographical time happen in the course of centuries and, hence, are almost imperceptible. The second level of time comprises social and cultural history, with social groupings, empires and civilizations. Change at this level (*histoire conjoncturale*) is much more rapid than in the first. The third level of time is *histoire événementielle*. This is the history of personalities, politics and exceptional events, such as war. Traditional history mostly takes into account only this third level. The history of events is conditioned by the two other levels underlying them. To the Annales School, everyday material life constitutes an impersonal deep-lying structure within which the history of grand action takes shape, the former dwarfing the latter. Also see Fernand Braudel, *The Structures of Everyday Life: The Limits of the Possible*.
5   Spengler opposes Faustian monotheism to Greek polytheism. He is of the view that Magian culture is not monotheistic; it was the Faustian man who transformed Magian Judaeo-Christianity. Remember Yahweh's struggle for supremacy with Baal, Marduk and other gods.
6   Spengler's point is that in the classical Greek tragedy, personality is a constant, and the crash of fortunes is the result of an inherent flaw, of the jealousy of gods or of chance, whereas the Faustian tragedy invokes the dynamic element of striving and suffering.
7   Polyphony suggests infinite space, which produces an effect beyond the capacity of individual elements in Pythagorean combinations. To Spengler, music is the dominant Faustian art.
8   According to Spengler, the world-feeling of a culture cannot be altered, and true conversion, strictly speaking, is impossible.
9   Soul-space is an analogue of boundless world-space.
10 Printing was, of course, independently invented by the Chinese as well, along with the compass, paper, gunpowder, telescope and porcelain.
11 This is the aspired move from the *fixum* to the *novum*, in Ernst Bloch's terminology. See Bloch 1986, 201.

12 Spengler was probably inspired by the Wagnerian opera *Götterdämmerung*, the twilight of the gods. The equivalent concept in Scandinavian mythology is *Ragnarök*.
13 In its encounter with the other, labelling and stereotyping are the mind's some of the many effort-saving devices.
14 See Jibu Mathew George, *The Ontology of Gods*, Chapter 6, especially the section entitled 'Self-Shifting Symmetry'.
15 Ontology is the branch of metaphysics that deals with the nature of being. It studies what entities exist or may be said to exist, how they may be classified and the more fundamental question of 'what does it mean to be'.
16 Deism restricted the deity to creation and envisioned a universe that works on its own uniform and impersonal laws.
17 Using a phrase borrowed from Friedrich Schiller, 'Disenchantment of the World' (*Entzauberung der Welt*), Weber outlined a process which Western civilization had been experiencing for several millennia and reached a high point with the scientific revolutions of modernity. In Weber's work, the phrase denotes, on the one hand, a development within the domain of religion from magic to paths to salvation completely devoid of magic and, on the other, an understanding of the world's occurrences increasingly by reference to natural forces, which are humanly controllable by rational calculation, physical laws and mechanical principles than to magical and supernatural powers (Weber 2005, xxii–xxiii). The second of the two senses is what matters to the present discussion.

Chapter 2

IF LITERATURE WERE TO DISAPPEAR FROM THE SPECTRUM OF DISCIPLINES ...

2.1 Why Do Things with Texts?

As students, some of us, at least during a brief phase of our education, have been part of a peer culture which cultivates belief in a disjunction between what happens inside the classroom and the life outside, except, of course, as one of the stepping stones to a career (Learning is earning!). This belief is the subversive subtext of all classroom interactions except of those which guarantee immediate 'entertainment'. But the professional practitioner of a discipline does not have this luxury. If she/he is asked why it should be studied at all, it does not suffice to amend Seneca, who criticized armchair philosophers, and platitudinize: *Non scholae sed vitae discimus* (we do not study for the school, but for life). A teacher of the assortment of traditional and contemporary texts which we continue to call literature, who is conscious of the nature of the discipline, will not be able to imagine teaching it without finding at least tentative answers to the question 'Why is it studied/taught?'. When a student of literature remarks that a classroom discussion 'goes over my head', except in cases of the ideological objection,[1] it is not only a matter of incomprehension but also of contestable relevance. More often than not, the 'So what?' which seeks a rationale is often an undiscerned supplement to the 'What?' of incomprehension. If literary studies were to disappear from the spectrum of academic disciplines, would we really miss something? Or, would we continue to do the myriad of things we do now, even in the absence of a label? Can disciplines exist without reflecting on why they exist and how they are organized? Even if the answer is in the affirmative, literature is certainly not one among those disciplines. Literary studies are a discipline which has a rich precedent of critical self-consciousness. There is no clearer indicator of this self-consciousness than the sophisticated and effervescent debate which problematizes its very subject matter – notions of what qualifies as 'literature'.

In any discipline, an adequate understanding of the object of study and a reflection on what exactly one can do with it determine the nature of study itself. One needs to ask if there are domain-specific canons of reasoning. If there are, must we pay heed to them, especially in the contemporary academic ambience of 'radical doubt'? What is a eureka moment for literary research? There is only one way of evading these questions in literature: be content with a set of random observations which we may designate 'phatic criticism'. The questions of what, why and how pertaining to the discipline indeed have a bearing on the processes and criteria by which students are admitted to various academic programmes, especially research programmes; the way their performance is evaluated and even on the decisions of selection committees for faculty recruitment. How can one *evaluate* without at least a vague conception of 'critical *values*', however relative they are, or without making explicit one's own assumptions concerning them? Let us consider these questions in a structured but inclusive and open-minded fashion – in a manner of intertextual informality.

2.2 Is 'Life' a Humanist Abstraction?

To the question 'Why literature?', the oft-mentioned scholarly points centre on language (a special use of it; also self-referential in the case of avant-garde modernism), imagination (as opposed to fact) and emotion. Besides these 'academic' characteristics of literature, the repeated, and trite sounding, reply given is: 'It tells us something about life'. The operative word, for the time being, is *life*. One often also hears adjectives such as 'life-enhancing' and phrases such as 'quality of life' in similar contexts. But under a poststructuralist/New Historicist paradigm, we are told that 'life' is a 'humanist abstraction'. The retreat of literary studies into a narcissistic world of professional word games might give credence to this view that it is out of tune with *real* life. And *experience* of life is no longer considered an individual or autonomous experience. In fact, we are so petrified by proclamations on the mediated character of 'experience' that we have come to prefer, *mutatis mutandis*, the less-reviled German words instead – *Erfahrung* and *Erlebnis*. Though it is possible to proceed to clarify the rationale for literary studies without dealing with the conceptual questions involved, in the interest of clarity, let us not, however, skip this step. What is the ontological status of the so-called abstractions?

The vocabulary of any language consists of a hierarchy of concepts. On the top of the hierarchy are macro-concepts (the concept of life, here). These are generalized ideas whose particular manifestations are expressed using micro-concepts (e.g., a life of suffering). These micro-concepts function as macro-concepts to concepts which are still lower in the hierarchy. In the above example, one might ask: what kind of suffering? The answer to the question (e.g., poverty, starvation, confinement, torture or destitution) is the corresponding micro-concept to the macro-concept immediately above in the hierarchy. The lower one moves down the hierarchy, the more particular the reference becomes. Literary realities are particularized ramifications or instantiations of concepts. When one looks from the top of the hierarchy, one can see only abstractions. This is inevitable as these are abstracted from concrete, particular instances of what the concept signifies in literature or experience. The macro-concept bears only an inadequate 'trace' of the particular experience. This is the case with an abstraction such as life as well. If, alternatively, one chooses to talk about 'love' and goes on to make statements about love in general, the exercise might hardly capture the concrete experience of any particular pair of lovers. Each love experience is unique and depends upon the nature of lovers.

Assuming that not all readers are resigned to the critical climate which brands life (or similar concepts) a mere humanist abstraction, let us ask ourselves: What aspect of life does literature reveal? What kind of knowledge does it impart? Before we answer this question let us survey some past formulations on the 'functions' of literature. Literature has often been understood from a non-utilitarian perspective, as a non-pragmatic discourse. Its 'use-lessness' is an idea which has been prevalent since the beginning of criticism. As Richard Eldridge points out:

> Any account of truth in poetry [including other genres of literature] must begin by facing the fact that poems are artifacts made neither for any immediate practical-material purpose, such as the satisfaction of bodily needs, nor with reference to measurements of material realities. Aristotle marks this difference between poems and other things by calling them imitations (*mimemata*) that are products of *poiesis*, as opposed either to actions that are products of *praxis* or accounts (*logoi*) that are products of *theoria*. (2010, 385)

If it does not serve any practical purpose, if it is use-less, why do we still cling on to it? But the discourse concerning the 'use' or 'uselessness' of literature implies functions of a different order than what these words suggest in common parlance. In the Wittgensteinian idiom, it is a different 'language-game' altogether, in the sense a different function of language is involved. Whether pushpin is 'of equal value with' (not 'as good as', as in John Stuart Mill's misquotation of Jeremy Bentham) poetry has to do not with variety in individual taste but with the difference in function. Aristotle (1920) himself assigned to literature the function – perhaps the oldest in the history of literary theory – of presenting the universal through the particular: 'By a universal statement I mean one as to what such or such a kind of man will probably or necessarily say or do'. Aristotle allowed for the mimesis (imitation) of things 'either as they were or are, or as they are said or thought to be or to have been, or as they ought to be'. Neoclassical critics followed this dictum. In his 'Preface to Shakespeare' (1765), Samuel Johnson termed ideal literary objects 'just representations of general nature'. Even Wordsworth, the Romantic, maintained, though from an almost diametrically opposite perspective, that the 'object' of poetry 'is truth, not individual and local, but general, and operative' (1800).

For centuries classical criticism thought literature capable of imparting instruction and causing delight, instruction through delight. The Romantics recognized it as capable of emotional orientation. John Stuart Mill, a Victorian, quite explicitly stated that the object of poetry was to act upon emotions: 'The delineation of states of feeling'. Though the modernists, in general, were understood as wary of emotion, T. S. Eliot in *The Sacred Wood* (1920) and F. R. Leavis in *Revaluation* (1936) wrote about a work of literature as 'a vehicle through which we rehearse various emotions, and by rehearsing acquire them [...] as dispositions which will eventually show themselves in actions' (qtd. in Scruton 2010, 98). The self-conscious modernist project of 'making it new' demonstrated that literature could reinvigorate the greatest of human gifts, language, preventing it from becoming stale.

Much has been said about the educational power of literature, its public function. If Abraham Lincoln greeted Harriet Beecher Stowe saying 'So this is the little lady who started this great war [the American Civil War],' he had good reasons for saying so. Literature has been widely recognized as an instrument of social change, an agent of historical transformation. In fact, this was so taken for granted that the impotency of literature in 'preventing' the two world wars enraged writers – a rage out of which avant-garde modernism and postmodernism were born, and threw literary art into a crisis – a crisis from which it never recovered, a crisis which irreversibly unsettled age-old conceptions of man, the world and language. Contemporary philosophers such as Martha Nussbaum (2004) would claim that literature sensitizes us ethically and emotionally for ordinary life. For Jenefer Robinson, the 'ability to understand emotionally' what characters experience is 'an asset in our attempts to understand fictional characters [her examples are Dorothea Brooke and Lambert Strether] as well as actual people' (2010, 81). Literature enables us to imagine experiences and undergo what we may call 'empathetic learning'. With Bernhard Schlink's *Der Vorleser* (*The Reader*) as a case in point, Mitchell Green shows how a literary work also prompts us to re-examine our entrenched beliefs (2010). Reading literature is also called an end or a reward in itself. Also available, at least since the modernists, Marcel Proust, in particular, is the anti-mimetic idea that 'life imitates art' (originally formulated by Oscar Wilde). Besides, we have the more experientially popular escapist theory of literary art. According to the escapist theory, reading is a picnic in another world, where we find temporary solutions to our ennui and exhaustion. Though the world of literature is that of make believe, it supplements the real world in many ways. But the problem is that none of these formulations may be true of all literary works across the board. Perhaps, we can never have one. Most of my own examples are drawn from twentieth-century fiction. As far as the impact – psychological, ethical, spiritual and so on – of literature upon human personality is concerned, to those who say that Wordsworth's poems helped John Stuart Mill recover from depression, the retort is that the SS guards at Auschwitz and Buchenwald read Goethe.

Since the advent of ideological criticism, literature has come to be seen as a 'power-ful' instrument for ideological conditioning, for the creation and inculcation of cultural norms and types which conform to the interests of the ruling classes. For Marxist critics, even when art is recognized as a refuge from tumultuous historical forces, as an isolated sphere of creativity, it is amenable to ideological redeployment. Literature was supposedly the domain of transcendental truths, eternal verities, as opposed to 'historical trivia' (Eagleton 1996, 22). The former could be the ideal space for ideological conditioning: a conservative historical status quo could be elevated to the former category. Literature is not a neutral entity but a political instrument, deeply implicated in discourses of power.

That literature has been an ideological instrument is not, however, the primary reason for studying it though students who are initiated into literary studies through ideological criticism might receive an impression to the contrary. Indeed, the discovery concerning the ubiquitous entanglement of entities previously believed to be neutral, in discourses which involve relations of power was a breakthrough. To be sure, there is nothing innocent under the sun, and knowledge is inevitably contested. But ideological criticism does not tell us: 'Study literature, it is significant'. It says: 'You studied it earlier as an innocent and detached entity; it is actually part of the foxy world. It may not be surreptitious, or part of a conspiracy; but it is the way it is. Therefore, study it closely to understand its networks of entanglement'.

As the foregoing discussion demonstrates, literary texts are closely related to the world in so many ways. Only we need a creative conception of the world and a sensitive articulation of the connections. Literature seems to be *the only discipline to be concerned, in equal measure, with both the word and the world* in the strictest sense. The following three sections will discuss the subtleties of the word-world connection in terms of a threefold rationale: *delicate epistemes*, *templates of significance* and *world-appetite*.

2.3 Delicate Epistemes of Literature

Clearly, literature makes a statement about the world, whether the scale be universal or particular. But what aspect of the world does it make this statement about? What is literary knowledge a knowledge of? An example given by Eagleton to illustrate the arbitrariness of defining literature is, though tangentially, of great import to us. According to Eagleton, literature is non-pragmatic discourse and 'any bit of writing may be read "non-pragmatically"': 'If I pore over the railway timetable not to discover a train connection but to stimulate in myself general reflections on the speed and complexity of modern existence, then I might be said to be reading it as literature' (1996, 8). Why and how do general reflections on the speed and complexity of modern existence constitute literature? These reflections pertain to something which needs to be reckoned and reflected on standing back from the pragmatic imperatives of life. Literature reveals something which is not so obvious, something which might miss us if we are not prepared for it. When we perceive something like this, we know that we are in the presence of literature. I propose to call this knowing a matter of *delicate epistemes*.[2] Literature is an endeavour which validates, or at least accommodates, delicate epistemes.

Let me illustrate the concept of delicate epistemes. In Bernhard Schlink's *The Reader* (1997), students of law discuss the belated trial of Nazi prison guards (the example here follows the film adaptation of *The Reader* (2008), directed by Stephen Daldry; the corresponding passage in the novel is slightly different). Hannah Schmitz, with whom Michael Berg, one of the students, has had an adolescent affair, is one among the accused. Berg is conscious of the subtle connections among diverse realities – livelihood (Hannah Schmitz was working for Siemens before she enlisted in the SS), precarious choices of ordinary Germans under the Nazi regime, love, guilt, duty and humanity. He articulates the subtleties in a language which is inadequate to convey them: 'We are trying to understand'. To his interlocutor's moral outrage, it is an open-and-shut case: 'What is there to understand?' Schlink's point is that the Jews and the ordinary Germans were both victims, though in different ways, and this knowledge will elude us if we are not sensitive to the subtleties of lived *life*. The point is also the difference between the two positions: 'What is there to understand?' and 'We are trying to understand'. Ironically, the question is affirmative, and the affirmative sentence opens up questions. The second position recognizes delicate realities, a recognition which is hard to come by.

The object of delicate knowledge is something which we are often compelled to be apologetic about in the face of logical fastidiousness. It is not easily amenable to rational demonstration or empirical verification. More often than not, it is suspect as valid knowledge. It is a kind of reality which can resist easy subsumption under readymade concepts. It is vulnerable to the charge of stating the obvious. It is known only through creative, intuitive and sensitive experience. It belongs to the realm of a simplicity that demands an audacity to believe in. It may be reduced to the level of the phatic. Adjectives such as 'silly', 'trivial', 'foolish', 'gaseous', 'vague', 'vacuous', 'self-indulgent' and 'cloying' may easily be applied to it. Jerome Stolnitz's essay dealing with the question of knowledge in literature is interestingly titled 'On the Cognitive *Triviality* of Art' (2004; emphasis added). We are apt to identify this delicate knowledge with the banal. It is that reality which evokes a sceptical 'What?' or 'So what?' It is the elusive referent of our careless, impatient pronoun 'whatever'. The strength of literature lies in its ability to deal with delicate realities. Henry James characterizes the implied perceiver of such a reality as 'one of the people on whom nothing is lost' (qtd. in Worthen 2005, 320). In order to apprehend it we need what André Gide calls *disponibilité* – a conscious openness to all kinds of experiences,[3] a receptiveness which John Keats suggested by the term 'negative capability', a capacity to be 'in uncertainties, mysteries, doubts, without any irritable reaching after fact and reason' (1992, 494).

The semantic field of the phrase 'delicate reality' is broad. Subtle realities of inner life – feelings, moods, whims and fancies – belong to this category. So do the delicate and often inscrutable aspects of relationships and the unlikely connections among divergent aspects of life. The delicate is delicate for many reasons. One, it is unobvious and can escape the experiencing subject without effort of a special kind. Two, it is not fully open to conceptual understanding. Three, it is not easily amenable to articulation.

The interiority of being, one of the delicate realities, has been a major concern of literary artists. Virginia Woolf, a writer who successfully utilized the medium of fiction to represent inner reality intimately, responds imaginatively to the interiority of another when in *The Waves* (1931) she makes Bernard reflect, 'I can never read a book in a railway carriage without asking, "Is he a builder? Is she unhappy?"' (1992, 61). In *Jacob's Room* (1922), she draws our attention to the subtle potential for destruction lurking in the quotidian: 'It's not catastrophes, murders, deaths, diseases, that age and kill us; it's the way we look and laugh, and run up the steps of omnibuses'. These words acquire new significance when seen in retrospect against the bombing of Bloomsbury and Woolf's own psychiatric problems. In *Mrs Dalloway* (1925), Septimus Warren Smith, a World War I veteran suffering from deferred traumatic stress, succumbs to the tragedy of living in a world that does not recognize what happens inside a man's head. His suicide affirms that the inner world is more important than the empirical world outside.

To revert to an earlier example from literary history, to his mother Gertrude's question about why his grief over the death of his father 'seems so particular with thee', Hamlet responds,

> Seems, madam? Nay, it is. I know not 'seems'.
> 'Tis not alone my inky cloak, good mother,
> Nor customary suits of solemn black,
> Nor windy suspiration of forc'd breath,
> No, nor the fruitful river in the eye,
> Nor the dejected 'haviour of the visage,
> Together with all forms, moods, shapes of grief,
> That can denote me truly. These indeed seem,
> For they are actions that a man might play.
> But I have that within which passeth show,
> These but the trappings and the suits of woe.
> (*Hamlet*, Act II, Scene II, lines 76–86)

As Martin Halliwell and Andy Mousley note,

> Hamlet's initial response, 'Seems, madam? Nay it is', suggests that the outward manifestation of his grief does 'denote [...] truly' the way he is feeling. Here being and seeming coincide. The rest of the speech, however, sees a rift between signs and psyche, public and private, outer and inner worlds. Outward signs thereby become inexpressive, and Hamlet turns away from these inauthentic exteriors into an interior world which is only partly accessible to others. (2003, 24–25)

In *Inwardness and Theater in the English Renaissance*, Katharine Eisaman Maus suggests that the 'alienation or potential alienation of surface from depth' in *Hamlet* and Renaissance culture often presented itself in the sceptical question 'of how to know what [other minds] are thinking' (1995, 5, 7). We can relate the *Hamlet* passage to our own times – the postmodern age – where being and seeming do not coincide, where the rift between signs and psyche, public and private, outer and inner worlds may even be an unwritten norm. Professedly, there are no depths, only surfaces – in Hamlet's idiom, only forms and shapes. Performativity conceptually overshadows what acts and expressions are a performance of. Obviously, this is not to say that men and women do not feel anything these days, especially about what happens to others, though one may be reminded of funerals wherein relatives and friends put on solemn appearances for the lengthy religious services or other rituals but as soon as the body is lowered into the grave turn to conversations of the following kind: 'You sold your Jaguar? What did you buy instead? A Ferrari?'

Our age is widely considered one of spectacle and sensation. When an accident is reported to passengers in a bus, they look out of the window and pull their neck back disappointed that the injury is not as severe as expected. The dynamics of spectacle operates by an aesthetic of frenzy. Media reports of accidents and human rights violations satisfy our sensation hunger with replayed virulence and intensity and provide us with simulations of the momentous, feebly replicating the negative enchantment of the original experience. Paradoxically, the age is also one which encourages passive, transient and homogenized responses to such events. This paradoxical blend of spectacle and passivity can be discerned in the 'cultural casts' available to individuals. We just need to fit into the casts regardless of what our commitments and engagements are. We are conditioned to be momentarily shocked. We are trained in the language of shock, in automatic but transient cathexis.[4] The casts give us an idiom to speak, tropes to repeat and a mould and a rationale to organize our feelings. The casts ensure that the semiotic of appearances pragmatically suffices for social life. Is there nothing beneath the semiotics, however inaccessible or inarticulable it maybe? Literature may have some answers.

Tereza's characterization of uniformly nude dream figures in Milan Kundera's *The Unbearable Lightness of Being* (1984) conveys yet another delicate reality which is neither easily accessible nor amenable to facile articulation: 'Theirs was the joyful solidarity of the soulless. The women were pleased at having thrown off the ballast of the soul – that laughable conceit, that illusion of uniqueness – to become one like the next' (2004, 35). Such observations gain credence if sensitivity and openness are the criteria. Fastidious propositional logic and empirical verification banish them from the purview of our consideration. The human world is so intriguing and one of so many entanglements that speculations concerning it, as said earlier, can imperceptibly stray into the region which has been traditionally called metaphysics. Knowledge of the human world is tantalizingly ever away – a knowledge which we fumblingly aspire to have in the documents of its experience. A conscious attempt to grasp the reality of the human cosmos can at best be characterized metaphorically as 'a sickle cast into the dark'. It may or may not find its unknown target in the trial-and-error journey, a humbling realization that makes us accept that knowledge of the proliferent, elusive human world process can only be an abstraction (see Chapter 1).

Artists have had access to delicate realizations in moments of illumination, which are a catchy version of delicate knowledge. In literary history, epiphanies have been gateways to the subtle realizations of the kind we have been discussing. James Joyce composed a series of prose sketches which he called 'Epiphanies' mostly between 1900 and 1903. In them he recorded scenes of ordinary life with delicate care. He made use of many of them in his later works. Joyce's epiphanies are often compared to Arthur Rimbaud's 'Illumination', Virginia Woolf's 'Moments of Being', Stéphane Mallarmé's 'instants of enchantment' and what Joseph Conrad calls 'moments of awakening'.[5] Endowed with openness to external stimuli and acute perceptiveness 'to pierce to the significant heart of everything' (Joyce 1956, 37), Stephen Dedalus, Joyce's autobiographical protagonist, experiences his epiphanies. As Morris Beja observes, although Joyce does not say that epiphanies can arise only from an insignificant and irrelevant object, all the epiphanies he recorded imply it (1971, 17). The 'vulgarity of speech or of gesture' or 'a memorable phase of the mind' is capable of achieving 'a sudden spiritual manifestation'. The 'soul' of the commonest object, 'its whatness leaps to us from the vestment of its appearance' (Joyce 1956, 216). During an epiphany commonplace phenomena receive an amplification that is not available under the workaday perspective. Stephen considers these moments 'evanescent' (218) for two reasons. First, the sensitive state of mind which apprehends the 'triviality' may be lacking later. Secondly, epiphanic scenes are particular instances of generic life processes. Although the generic process goes on, the particular case may not recur. Stephen's epiphanies include a colloquy overheard in Eccles Street (where Joyce was to house Leopold and Molly Bloom later in *Ulysses*) between a young lady and a gentleman (1956, 216) and the string of three scenes in *A Portrait of the Artist as a Young Man* each beginning with 'he was sitting' (67–68). The later epiphanies in *A Portrait*, such as that of the bird-like girl wading on the seashore (171–72), are presented as a prelude to Stephen's choice of an artistic vocation.

We are intuitively aware that there is something in the following passage from Vladimir Nabokov's *Lolita* which is beyond categories that enjoy currency:

> A normal man given a group photograph of school girls or Girl Scouts and asked to point out the comeliest one will not necessarily choose the nymphet among them. You have to be an artist and a madman, a creature of infinite melancholy, with a bubble of hot poison in your loins and a super-voluptuous flame permanently aglow in your subtle spine (oh, how you have to cringe and hide!), in order to discern at once, by ineffable signs – the slightly feline outline of a cheekbone, the slenderness of a downy limb, and other indices which despair and shame and tears of tenderness forbid me to tabulate – the little deadly demon among the wholesome children; she stands unrecognized by them and unconscious herself of her fantastic power. (1982, 10–11)

Indeed, Nabokov's work is an intertextual evocation of literary tropes from all across literary history (not only Edgar Allan Poe's poem 'Annabel Lee'). The above-quoted statement of Humbert Humbert, the paedophile-parent-lover (he is also a literary scholar!), opens up a vast realm of subtle realities: shame, melancholy, despair, art and madness as conditioning factors in the paradoxical blend of choosing love objects and hesitating to explore the choice. Probably, a parallel obtains between choice of love objects and choice of books, a thread which we shall pick up again when we discuss reader-text symmetry.

To those who claim that the reading of Goethe did not make the SS guards sensitive, one can point out the hardening of *epistemes* that made the structures of German political and popular thought blind to the reality of the other. Nazism and the Holocaust were phenomena which crushed everything delicate under the juggernaut of a hyper-sturdy state. Jewish life simply did not matter. As countless Nazi propaganda films and Art Spiegelman's graphic novel *Maus* (1986) show, Jews were mere mice or maggots. That the SS guards attended Sunday services, had a great time with the family and read Goethe before stoking up the fire which burnt human flesh demonstrates the inscrutable complexity of life, and demands a more complex explanation for the Holocaust.

In a fastidious epistemic setup, one is likely to dismiss Wordsworth's poetical statement 'The Child is father of the Man' as a logical paradox, thereby passing over a nuanced understanding of the human life trajectory by which a child's qualities are a necessary precursor to those of adulthood. There ought to be an order of referential or quasi-referential connections, and a system of knowledge, particularly in disciplines that deal with objects of study marked by what we have called an ontology of the intangible, which enables us to recognize delicate truths and even more delicate ways of enunciating them. In a world of facile generalizations and instant dismissals, where words fail to signify, where habitual scepticism is mistaken for critical intelligence, the imperative of all knowledge is to supplement the *hermeneutic of epistemic fastidiousness* (a hermeneutic that 'filters out') with a *hermeneutic of delicate epistemes* (a hermeneutic that 'lets in'). The latter involves sensitization to unarticulated, subtle and diverse realities of experience (e.g., children's perceptions). At least in literary studies rigor and sympathy are not necessarily antithetical. In fact, other disciplines have corresponding instances of productively envisaged 'epistemic loosening' – for example, Arthur Versluis's concept of 'sympathetic empiricism' (qtd. in Lowry 2017, xxviii), which was developed to deal with esoteric doctrines. Who can rule out an order of reality in which such a description of the world as 'All is Brahman' (the maxim of *Advaita*, or non-dualism) corresponds to its referent as exactly as Newton's laws of motion? We know how to filter out knowledge with fastidious epistemes; we also need to know how to let in unprivileged knowledge.

Is the delicate reality a part of the world? Or, is it all in the experiencing subject? In the history of thought we are past the Realist–Idealist debate, and there is no point in jealously attributing the epiphany of the delicate exclusively to either the subject or the object. This awareness of reality is a singular conjunction of both nature and art, of the subject and the object, of language and phenomenon, of the word and the world. Writers struggle to express complex and elusive realities in the sign-systems at their disposal. Readers read into the network of signifiers their own. Romanticism resulted from the inadequacy of readymade diction (in Neoclassicism) to convey the reality it wanted to. Avant-garde modernism too emerged, among other things, as a response to the epistemic inadequacy of the static, stable, mainstream common sense of Victorian modernity and its crises with regard to apprehension and representation of reality.

Delicate realities of literature are made in language. The mirror metaphor is inadequate here; language may not be a mirror held up to a *pre-existent* reality. One may still wonder whether these singular perceptions of reality merely reach the reader in the form of dispensable 'inflections' in language? No. For a parallel example, William James notes how the different names of wines help us discriminate their subtly different flavours far more clearly than we could without the use of such names (qtd. in Shusterman 2010, 12). The inseparability of form and content is an old idea in criticism. It is not surprising that New Criticism, one of the schools which argued for this inseparability, also assigned literature 'a special role'. Many things happen at the convergence of the word and the world. The 'what' of the complex referent, especially in a world of intangibles, and the 'how' of enunciation are interdependent to such an extent that we may call the result a verbal epiphany and nothing else. It is not for nothing that figures of speech are placed at the disposal of literary discourse. No wonder rules of discourse have been traditionally made lax for it, which was also partly responsible for earning literary studies the ignominy of a soft discipline. With an infinitely large number of potential neologisms and morphological combinations, language has exponential possibilities of representation. It is not for nothing that criticism concerns itself with both the word and the world. It is possible for figurative language to represent even physical realities in a way (here, anthropomorphic) that adds meaning resonances (e.g., the characterization of cancer as a phenomenon in which a cell goes mad and destroys the rest).

How does one relate the concept of delicate epistemes to the universal/local and historical/transcendent debates pertaining to defining literature? We must be willing to concede that delicate truths might not have universal validity. The formulation might not even be true of all literature. What is delicate and needs articulation might vary from age to age and from culture to culture. Viola's words to Olivia – 'Lady, you are the cruel'st she alive, / If you will lead these graces to the grave, / And leave the world no copy' (*Twelfth Night*, Act I, Scene V, lines 225–27) – could have a different impact on a people whose ideas of time, mutability and procreation are different from those of the Elizabethans. Similarly, an idle set of people who have throughout their life span more-than-ample time to harp on all kinds of banal matters might not need literature in this sense at all.

The relationship of delicate epistemes to the popular theme of social emancipation is interesting. Though a lot of what we have been discussing may sound 'canonical', that the concept is not always elitist is clear from the following anecdote, which made me think of a corresponding concept. A student once said that in her childhood, an extremely deprived one, she thought that green grapes (so pure, lush, succulent and attractive) were 'not meant' for 'ordinary people'. The marginalized sections of society have a higher stake in the delicate because it is their realities that can easily be brushed aside. Strangely, the historical elitism of genres also collapses before the delicate. Are there genres which are particularly suitable for conveying the delicate knowledge? Arguably, it is not possible to make a priori observations on the efficacy of genres in this regard. Theoretically, any genre is capable of this. The blog, the most recent arrival at the gates of the canon of genres, might well be able to perform the task as efficaciously as the epic.

Before we conclude this section, let me illustrate, with the help of Günter Grass's *The Tin Drum* (1959), the significance of delicate realities in the face of harrowing historical experience. Having lived under excruciating historical conditions, Grass, in his fictional writings, salvages the 'little experiential truths' that could easily be crushed under the juggernaut of a hyper-sturdy Nazi state and a catastrophic war, or brushed aside by historical transformations which threatened to subsume life trajectories of ordinary people (*kleine Leute*, in the terminology of *Alltagsgeschichte*, history of everyday life). It is productive to read Grass in retrospect against the hardening of *epistemes* which made the structures of German political and popular thought insensitive to the 'the other', in that it provides a fecund critical framework to understand the multidimensionality of his political 'engagement'. His choice of child narrators, his unapologetic emphasis on trivia, his use of magic realism (particularly given the scepticism surrounding the efficacy of fiction and fantasy to 'do justice' to historical experience) and his deployment of the weird suggest a conscious attempt to capture and resuscitate singular, elusive human realities in the face of menacingly enveloping macro-historical developments. The psychological basis for this claim is that when conditions of existence become overwhelming or unbearably harrowing, human consciousness develops a compensatory tendency to utilize even the smallest possibilities.[6]

Grass makes Oskar Matzerath, a perpetual child, the narrator of German history. This is significant in that children are the least-accounted historical subjects. Being a midget, an inversion of the Bambino, Oskar also typifies the *Untermensch* (the subhuman), a perversely appropriated Nazi antithesis to Nietzsche's *Übermensch*. He is under constant threat of the ongoing T-4 forced euthanasia programme. Mr Bebra warns Oskar of the leaders who would 'preach our destruction' 'down from the rostrums' (Grass 1961, 110) and asks him to sit down rather than stand and reveal the height. Grass filters history through little Oskar's eyes, which enables him to dwell upon delicate realities, and enunciate them in even more delicate ways. Oskar narrates the unfolding grand history in terms of how it impinges on his apparently insignificant preoccupations, the tin drum being the most potent symbol in this regard. As a book, *The Tin Drum* seems to suggest that the destiny of these least-reckoned of history's subjects is the sphere where the effects of historical forces are most registered, and in Grass's revisionist historiography is made the criterion to evaluate the desirability of the latter. What is most significant about Grass's ordinary history is the inversion of priorities: repair of drums, playing of cards, the fizz powder, Jan Bronski's stamp collection, the eels wriggling in salt and observation of ants are greater concerns than the fate of Poland. Of course, there have been narratives, literary and cinematic, which look at history through an innocent or deficient person's impish perspective – for example, Winston Groom's *Forrest Gump* (1994). Gump is slow-witted but athletically prodigious. In literary history, the impish, estranging perspective has been a favourite auctorial device to offer a critique of the status quo.

Little people (here, literally little!) have a higher stake in the delicate because it is their realities that are more vulnerable to being brushed aside or trampled under. Oskar's screaming and drumbeating are ways of drawing attention of the greater world to his own needs. Let me quote the passage narrating the pregnant Agnes's funeral:

> Before the coffin went Father Wiehnke with a sexton bearing incense. My eyes slipped from the back of Matzerath's neck to the furrowed necks of the pallbearers. I had to fight down a passionate desire: Oskar wanted to climb up on the coffin. He wanted to sit up there and drum. However, it was not his tin instrument but the coffin lid that he wished to assail with his drumsticks [...] He wanted to drum for the mourners who were repeating their prayers after Father Wiehnke. And as they lowered the casket into the ground, he wished to stand firm on the lid [...] He wished to go down into the pit with Mama and the foetus. And there he wished to remain while the survivors tossed in their handfuls of earth, no, Oskar didn't wish to come up, he wished to sit on the tapering

foot end of the coffin, drumming if possible, drumming under the earth, until the sticks rotted out of his hands, until his mama for his sake and he for her sake should rot away, giving their flesh to the earth and its inhabitants; with his very knuckles Oskar would have wished to drum a soft rhythm for the foetus, if it had only been possible and allowed. (Grass 1961, 159–60)

This is how language can poignantly cross the barrier between life and death. Perhaps this is also the only way a son can say that his mother was raped by Red Army soldiers[7] – this is the delicate episteme of literary art. Perhaps the whole tale of Agnes's promiscuous passion is a sublimated version of ubiquitous sexual violence during the War.

2.4 Templates of Significance

A second rationale of literature is that it furnishes the readers what we may call *templates of significance*. While delicate epistemes of literature salvage and foreground apparently insignificant, elusive and hard-to-articulate realities, literary templates help organize these amorphous realities into patterns of significance. The consciousness of an active recipient of literature is palimpsestic. A palimpsestic consciousness gains from art templates for quotidian predicaments, agonies and dilemmas – for everything which is otherwise branded as banal. Joyce's *Ulysses* (1922), an encyclopaedic inventory of the commonplace, amply illustrates the point. The book showcases culture (in the restricted sense of products of art and philosophy) as a repertoire of resources for daily life. Literary, liturgical and Biblical quotations, proverbs and snatches of songs punctuate the thoughts and words of characters. The words of philosophers give food for the day's thought. Culture caters to the imaginary of the everyday. Maria Cummins's romantic fiction compensates Gerty McDowell for a home destroyed by her father's alcoholism, her own bodily deformity and resultant social disadvantages. But above and beyond the traditional argument that art seeks to mitigate an unpleasant reality, images, ideas and verbal fragments from literary texts are enlisted to impart significance to personal events. For instance, Leopold Bloom, the protagonist and the everyman, uses words from Vincenzo Bellini's opera *La Sonnambula* (1831) 'All is lost now' (Joyce 1984, 11.22, 11.635, 14.1133)[8] to refer to the loss of his adulterous wife, Molly, to her concert manager, Hugh 'Blazes' Boylan. In *La Sonnambula* the heroine Amina walks into the seductive arms of Rodolf, who is, however, dissuaded by her innocence. The real cuckold who transforms the meaning of human affection, charity and freedom through his ordinary day (and night), but passes by without even being noticed, gains a significance from such associations. Similarly, Stephen, frustrated in his artistic ambitions (another frustrated artist named Adolf Hitler found other templates!) and unaccepted by the Dublin literati, echoes John Dryden's words to Jonathan Swift – 'Cousin Swift, you will never be a poet' – when he says to himself, 'Cousin Stephen, you will never be a saint' (3.128). Cultural history, especially its literary component, facilitates a quotidian form of archetypal role-playing. As Bloom's use of *La Sonnambula* and Stephen's use of Dryden's words demonstrate, archetypes, an important principle of modernist literature, serve as psychosocial aids to the everyday hermeneutic of the self and the other. Borrowed words, phrases, ideas and identities furnish frameworks over a new situation. They often help the characters fix the ambiguous meaning of a situation. The Romanian religious philosopher Mircea Eliade (1954) has drawn attention to the tendency of the religious men of archaic societies (*homo religiosus*), as opposed to the modern, secular man, to see the events of the present as gathering their significance from their fitting the patterns of a glorious past. These men see their own deeds as re-enactments of the deeds of gods, of ancient heroes and of illustrious ancestors. In Joyce's novel, characters and narrators invoke the archaic patterns playfully. Thus *homo religiosus* becomes *homo ludens* (playful man).

Literary representations console and convince us that quotidian predicaments, agonies and dilemmas are not banal. Non-events become literary events. A trivial conversation becomes an existentially profound conversation, or, at least, a repartee. Self-revulsion is appropriately sublimated into moral dilemma. Fleeting moments of banality are given 'a local habitation and a name'. The self through which many mundane events crisscross, gains a quasi-heroic status. Not mourning one's mother's death (Camus' *L'Étranger*) and the strange choice of a love object (Nabokov's *Lolita*) are installed in the realm of significant entities when 're-viewed' by art against the larger horizon of human existence and imagination. Life *can* imitate art. For an example from another genre, in the film *Troy* (2004) Achilles tells Briseis, the captured slave-turned-love, on the eve of the fatal battle: 'I'll tell you a secret. Something they don't teach you in your temple. The gods envy *us*. They envy us because we're mortal. Because any moment might be our last. Everything is more beautiful because we are doomed'. The statement appeals to mortals because it imparts significance to the absurdity of lovemaking on the eve of avoidable death. Achilles's oral meta-narrative creates literary templates of significance. Gratuitous suffering attains ritualistic grandeur.

2.5 World-Appetite

The third rationale for literature is what I call *world-appetite*.[9] The term is my supplement to *Weltschmerzen*, a term coined by the German author Johann Paul

Friedrich Richter (1763–1825) to denote 'world-pain' or 'world-weariness', a kind of feeling experienced by someone who understands that physical reality can never satisfy the demands of the human mind (sometimes also denoting the world's hostility to individual aspirations). Human capacity for world-comprehension fails to match up with world-appetite. Despite the dissatisfaction surrounding this, the appetite for the prolific world stays. 'Sensation hunger' is a sub-category of a more general world-appetite. We know that in many instances of its usage, the word 'world' connotes, and often stands for, *others*. Appetite for the world is primordially an appetite for the other. We want to be in the company of people who are like us. We are also curious about people who are unlike us. This perhaps explains the refusal of literary desires to remain parochial despite the political character of knowledge creation and 'nativist apologetics' of all hues (We shall discuss 'nativist apologetics' and the resultant ghettoization of knowledge in the final chapter). Radical otherness intensifies the world-appetite. In short, the world-appetite of a reader is the desire to be part of the life-world of others, or at least to have a glance at that world. In its mundane versions, it might make literature a bit voyeuristic and gossipy, though.[10]

World-appetite could be a passion for places which embody the force of life – and of art. Literary/historical tourism – pilgrimage, if you like – draws upon the desire to know the spaces and cultures which produced the art the world admires, or, conversely, the horror it shrinks from: Yeats's Sligo, the Lake District, Auschwitz, a slave quarter and so on. Herein lies the market value of contemporary cultural showcasing both in the art world and in academia. In *The Postcolonial Exotic: Marketing the Margins* (2001), Graham Huggan explains on the lines suggested by the title why the corporate publishing world co-opted postcolonial writing. World-appetite often manifests itself in literature as a *curiosity for the singular*. The idea is that people read because they would like to be enchanted by the new, the strange and the unique. A century ago, Leo Tolstoy gave us a clue to the singularity of life-worlds when he opened *Anna Karenina* with the following oft-quoted words: 'Happy families are all alike; every unhappy family is unlike in its own way' (1978, 1). Indeed, happiness can also be singular. It seems, however, that a sane, passionless and happy world is too flat for fiction.

There is a view abroad that 'good literature' (certainly, the good is largely subjective) is essentially uncanny. Harold Bloom's theory of the canonical work emphasizes singularity above every other quality, even above his thesis on the chain of successive anxieties that run down the line of literary artists across the ages: 'When you read a canonical work for a [*sic*] first time, you encounter a stranger, an uncanny startlement rather than a fulfilment of expectation' (1995, 3). The German word for uncanny, *unheimlich*, whose etymology

Sigmund Freud discusses in detail in his essay 'The Uncanny', means 'not of home'. In its modern usage, the uncanny is familiar and yet strange. The uncanny in literature pertains to both the word and the world. It could be the strangeness of the fictional world, of setting, of character, of world view, of diction, or a combination of these or other elements of a work.

Though apparently fantasy fiction has a greater potential to startle than realist fiction has, the spectrum extends from the magical world of fantasy, through the grotesque charms of the gothic, to the mundane in hyperrealist fiction (Leopold Bloom defecates in full view of the readers!).[11] Imaginative enchantment operates at subliminal levels, and no genre, text or technique is innately incapable of it. The source of startlement could be Joyce's linguistic vitality or encyclopaedic grasp, Henry James's intricate plots and twists therein, or Milan Kundera's singular visions or the nausea of Nana's smallpox-inflicted death in Zola's novel of the same name. The singularity might be a matter of the writer's perception and presentation. Reflecting in retrospect on the mimetic theory of art, M. H. Abrams writes,

> The objects or qualities are conceived to be inherent in the constitution of the universe, and the genius of the poet is explained primarily by his acuity of observation, enabling him to discover aspects of reality hitherto unregarded, and by his artistic ingenuity, enabling him to select and arrange even the more familiar elements into novel combinations which, nevertheless, surprise us by their truth. (1989, 8)

Russian formalists called this process 'defamiliarization'. It is often said that there are only a limited number of plots which will have to be re-circulated in 'novel' forms. Artistic appeal lies, then, in singular configurations.

Avant-garde modernism was quite explicit about what Ezra Pound called 'mak[ing] it new'. An Iranian student on my 'Twentieth-Century American Fiction' course once asked: 'I don't understand why you have prescribed *Three Lives*?' My answer then was: 'It was precisely to make you ask this question that Gertrude Stein wrote the book' (not to speak of *The Making of the Americans*). The 'difficult' art of the modernists, indeed, places itself beyond the reach of the common reader, an attitude expressed by Eugene Jolas in his pronouncement in the Paris-based journal *Transition*, 'the plain reader be damned' (qtd. in Ellmann 1983, 588n). According to Malcolm Bradbury and James McFarlane, modernist art represents 'a hoarding of the artistic powers against the populace' (1976, 28). The modernist 'aesthetic of shock' is meant to be a 'slap in the face'[12] of those who read Mills and Boon! But this self-consciously jarring, perplexing aesthetic of illogicality (with meta-literary implications in the case of avant-garde modernism, which showcased the armoury of art as well as its crisis), disconnections and uncanny happenings is part and parcel of all literary endeavour. Haven't we heard people using the phrase 'a taleless tale' for certain narratives? What they do not say but mean is that familiar concepts are inadequate to follow and appreciate these narratives.

Like delicate epistemes, singularity is also culturally relative. The contours of word-world-curiosity vary not only from one historical epoch to another and from one culture to another but also from person to person. If 'interpretive strategies' (Stanley Fish's term) are culturally acquired, and reading shares a 'horizon of expectations' (a term fundamental to Hans Robert Jauss's reception theory), why do readers with the same cultural background respond differently to the same texts? The ingredients of culture may be inherited and common, but at least their combinations are singular. As for historical change, at least to some of us the jarring aesthetic of avant-garde modernism is not a shock anymore. The new loses its punch! Nevertheless, as long as literature continues to denote and connote places, things, characters, events, emotions, perceptions and world views, it will not disappoint us. Age cannot wither it, nor custom stale its infinite variety. This is not to say that singularity is the only reason why people read books. There are other virtues, many other perfections!

2.6 Reader-Text Symmetry

We have seen that response to literary art (and perhaps all art) stems from a variety of needs on the affective-cognitive continuum. The nature of these needs, their modes of fulfilment and the kind of knowledge provided by literary texts condition the modes of interaction between the text and the reader. We have explained the response to literature in terms of three concepts: delicate epistemes, templates of significance and world-appetite. As hinted at in the course of the previous discussion, the reader-text interface has a strong subjective component. This concluding part endeavours to clarify the subjective dimension of this interface. It has been one of the perennial curiosities of my life to learn how others respond to a work of art – a book, a film, a piece of music or a painting. Why do we prefer some books to others? Though a more complex question, why do readers interpret texts differently? Could anything explain a reader's interest in particular texts, authors and epochs? What are the secrets of those private moments – Arundhati Roy called these moments 'vulnerable' – when we make our way in a fictional world? Not only meaning and interpretation, but our whole response, even the very decision to pick a book from the racks (provided we have a modicum of 'pre-understanding'), is a matter of experiential symmetry, real or imagined, between the text and ourselves.

The idea of symmetry has witnessed a dramatic change since the enthronement of the reader in the place of the 'dead' author. As Jenefer Robinson illustrates, 'If I read in a novel a description of a handsome young fighter-pilot who dies in the Second World War, and fall into a tender reverie about my fiancé who flies a plane for Fed-Ex, my feelings of tenderness may have nothing to do with the way the fighter-pilot is depicted in the novel' (2010, 71). Robinson's theory leans towards the subjective side of the reader-text interface. Contemporary literary theory is right to a great extent in hailing the text as a network of reciprocal effects. Texts *for us* are partly about themselves and partly about ourselves. The reader-text symmetry may be explained in terms of meaning or succour to our lives, intellectual stimulation, antidote to ennui and so on. In other words, the effects are a matter of encounter between the subject and the object. It is both constitutive of, and a result of, our *Lebenswelt*.

The encounter with the text is the cumulative climax of the reader's individual and collective experiences. The antecedents of this encounter include more factors than are often assumed. Many components synthesize and mutate to form our world view (and text-view) – heredity, history, tradition, codes, religion, class, caste, race, gender, location, education, linguistic and cultural repertoire, cultural and ethical norms, psychohistories, beliefs, interests, motives, tastes, moods, interpersonal relations, what others read (and watch), calculations, Facebook habits, childhood experiences and the spider and the moonlight. The last two are Nietzsche's items in his theory of eternal recurrence. Reading revives more ghosts than can be enumerated! Since many of these factors change in the course of a person's life, the symmetry is not a static one; it is a dynamic, shifting, progressive symmetry. As a result, we come to dislike texts which we liked in an earlier phase of life (a reaction formation?) and vice versa. Since the repertoire of factors listed above is partly cultural, the contours of the symmetry might shift as well on a collective scale. It is doubtful whether an allusive text may have as much impact in the age of the internet (the eleventh muse!) as high modernist ones had had.

The symmetry could be cognitive or affective, affirmative or contrastive. We might find confirmation of our beliefs in texts. We might agree with the text. We might allow the text to convince us, if our beliefs are different from its. We might quarrel with the text. We might pick up a text to refute it. We can read meanings into texts. We can also read out meanings that we prefer. Texts can both generate and violate expectations. We might use texts as partners in dialogue. It is one of today's critical truisms that reading, like other experiences, is culturally mediated. One end of the reader-text symmetry is controlled by market forces. Production of formulaic works is one of the many mechanisms by which what is offered is made to fit the other end of the symmetry. Readers might read a work because it carries prestige. As we know, both publishing firms and academia can 'hype' a work.

Despite the fact that we are part of a community of readers and our hermeneutic repertoire is mostly shared, we, as individual readers, are capable of singular syntheses. Conversely, we can also relate to texts from other cultures even if we have no experiential knowledge of their lived life. This is because the repertoires of cultures have so many elements in common. Goneril and Regan sound like Indian daughters (or daughters-in-law)! We 'concretize' cross-culturally, albeit in our own ways. The text will find its reader due to its textuality. 'Iterability' (Jacques Derrida's concept which describes the capacity of signs and texts to be repeated in new situations and to produce new meanings; 1982) at the other end of the symmetry is a celebration of the readers' worlds. Perhaps this is one reason why, despite the putative political bases of intellectual and aesthetic categories, despite centuries of familiarity with similar themes, literature has not disappeared.

Such symmetries and textualities are relevant beyond literary studies. Let me give an example from my recent studies in the philosophy of religion. Religious and quasi-religious (e.g., philosopher's God) schemata across epochs and cultures adumbrate in place of a monolithic idea of a supernatural being (or beings), a heterogeneous gamut of signifieds that correspond to a *God-signifier* – a continuum of varied God-ontologies (sometimes implicit): a personal being, a logical necessity, a universal intelligence, an impersonal cosmic force, shorthand for an underlying principle, a symbol of human perfections and a heuristic metaphor for the operative logic of the world process, which consists of cosmic, historical and personal trajectories, with intermediate metaphysical and quasi-metaphysical entities on a tropological continuum (George 2017, 34). History of religions represents an ideational movement along this continuum, a change from one tropology to another. From a long-temporal perspective, belief in a personal God or gods – supernatural entities with only a local influence being a fragmentary version of the cosmic narrative – is analysable as only one of the historically realizable possibilities on the continuum. Religious ideation can be studied in terms of *a matrix of dialectical correspondences* between God-conceptions of varied ontologies and historical experience, whereby a personal deity is considered *vital*, merely *conducive, compatible, redundant* or even *detrimental*. The ontological dynamism of religion offers the option of an experientially induced ideational movement along the ontological continuum, that is, a change in the idea of God – God in full control versus God as a nominal presiding or originating force, or even God as a symbol of concerns. When the subject encounters experience which contradicts the collectively or institutionally offered God-schema, the idea of a personal God who intervenes in every individual destiny can get diluted and may finally disappear in flexible alternative ideations. People might still 'believe in God', but this God could be little more than a vague force or a nominal power which, in view of the comprehensive ecclesiastical organization of faith and life, at least in the heyday of religion (as represented by medieval Christendom; see 1.6) is somehow made to correspond to the divine entity of traditional religion.

The aforementioned ideational movements along the ontological continuum are held in check by collective, institutional regulation, and religious dogma represents a historical solidification on the continuum. But owing to the indeterminacy of the object (the supernatural is unlike anything known in natural experience) and the free-ontological dynamism, illustrated above, embedded in religious ideation, human mediation offers unlimited prospects. Religious-institutional picture of the supernatural is only a first-order mediation – a second-order reality in itself. Religious subjects further mediate the product of this first-order mediation, scrutinizing and re-appropriating received ontologies. What these mediatory possibilities lead to is a *symmetric ontology*, wherein the 'being' of God/gods lies in the experientially induced and historically shifting symmetry – weak or strong – between ideation on the one hand and an epoch, group or individual subject on the other. Such a 'reception dynamic' is made possible by the fact that the ideational system is *a text*, which the religious subjects concretize in ways which are meaningful to them in their diverse and changing life contexts. An example of the textual capacity to appeal to a situation different from the text's origin (Derrida's *iterability*) is the second symmetric context (the first is the Babylonian captivity) of Daniel's prophesy – Israel's struggle against the Seleucid Empire. History of religion could well be a function of iterability – a *textualism of faith*.

Notes

1 Roland Barthes examines the intellectual false modesty involved in the tendency to dismiss non-traditional schools of thought such as Marxism and existentialism under the guise of incomprehensibility. See Roland Barthes, 'Blind and Dumb Criticism', in *Mythologies*, trans. Annette Lavers (London: Cape, 1972), pp. 33–34.

2 *Episteme* is Michel Foucault's term for historically specific norms of discourse that determine what can be accepted as valid knowledge. Of course, in the *Nichomachean Ethics* Aristotle made a distinction among *episteme* (theoretical knowledge), *technê* (craft) and *phronesis* (practical wisdom and ethics). To the ancient Greeks, the word *episteme*, from which we have the modern word epistemology, meant unvarying, universal knowledge, or 'justified true belief', which has been the condition of valid knowledge for quite some time. As is well known, epistemology is the branch of philosophy which deals with the theory of knowledge – the methods of acquiring knowledge, its validity and justification.

3 The character Michel in Gide's novel *L'Immoraliste* (1902; *The Immoralist*) embodies this quality.
4 The Freudian term 'cathexis' means investment of mental or emotional energy in a person, object or idea. 'Cathexis' is translator James Strachey's English word for Freud's German term *Besetzung*, which simply means interest.
5 See Beja (1971, 21), Brunsdale (1993, 95) and Frye (1957, 61).
6 Refer to the discussion of the relationship between extreme experience and creativity in 1.7.
7 In a 1978 interview to the French journalist Nicole Casanova, Grass revealed that his mother had been raped by Red Army soldiers when they conquered Danzig. He added that he would not have said that in German for another twenty years (qtd. in Preece 2009, 17).
8 In keeping with the tradition of using the Gabler edition of *Ulysses*, episode and line numbers are cited instead of page numbers.
9 The concept of world-appetite has certain affinities with what Ranjan Ghosh calls the 'hunger' ingrained in literature, or, more precisely, literature as hunger, though 'the world' is not an explicit concern for the latter. The hunger, by and large, manifests itself in the interpretive, explicatory, synthesizing and re-imagining ventures of man. In Chapter 9 of *Thinking Literature across Continents*, entitled 'The Ethics of Reading Sahitya', a reworked version of his earlier work 'Aesthetics of Hunger', Ghosh elaborates,

> The ethics of sahitya (literature) are inscribed in a variety of hunger. Sahitya creates its own hunger, the desire to feed on the 'other' and be fed upon. It is formed out of a hunger to explicate ways of human experience and engagements with emotions. It is anchored in a hunger that is its *eros*, its creative aesthesis, its power of sustenance and motivation. The inherent hunger of sahitya calls for at once imaginative ventures of crossdisciplinarity and the understanding of human values born out of philosophic designs, both conceptual and experiential. Sahitya has the ability to operate beyond the point of a direct act of perception. This is what lends freedom to individual interpretive journeys, furthering intelligible aesthetic experiences. We encounter new interpretive behaviors with potentially realizable values springing out of a certain premise of inheritance, a literary heritage, ideas nourished by a certain intellectual climate, cultural and symbolic accumulation, and also some unfulfillments that keep sahitya alive against the reificatory modes of subjugation. Hunger satiated is hunger generated. Hunger attended is hunger made possible. Hunger is experience realized; hunger is responsibility awaiting fulfillment. The ethics of sahitya argue for various incarnations of hunger, both at the level of the aesthetic and the postaesthetic. (2016, 207)

The affinities are more obvious than elsewhere when Ghosh discusses 'the other': 'this "aesthetic of hunger" in sahitya is about forming, foregrounding, and fictionalizing the "other". This other is born out of an urge and need to feel for a variety of discourses and thoughts across cultures and traditions' (208).
10 According to Ranjan Ghosh, 'The complex dynamics between hunger and the other throw us into the fury and force of literary cannibalism' (2016, 209).
11 *Ulysses* is at least partly hyperrealist – of course, in a self-reflexive way.
12 The allusion is to the title of the Russian Futurist manifesto 'A Slap in the Face of Public Taste' issued by Vladimir Mayakovsky and others in 1917.

Chapter 3

BEYOND FOR AND AGAINST: TENDENCIES OF CONTEMPORARY CRITICISM

3.1 What to Do with Texts?

As part of the ongoing 'transvaluation' of established literary values, we have successfully argued and accepted that texts, authors, genres and social groups other than the canonical ones ought to be studied as part of the syllabi. In other words, we are past the phase of 'restricted entry', and objects of study have democratically multiplied. But there has been no corresponding rethinking, at least to the same degree, on what more can be done with the old and the new entrants. Somehow, originality in research has come to mean writing theses and books on less-canonical works. When we decide merely to study less-known works (it is an open secret that first-generation critics have certain advantages), we are mainly questioning the canon, not necessarily devising *ways* of dealing with texts which have hitherto been excluded, though new texts may demand new approaches.

During my initial years as a research scholar, I was asked to read up the secondary materials on a certain author – 'a love that dare not speak its name' – other than James Joyce, on whose works I did my doctoral research, so as to have an overview of the then current trends in practical criticism. After a year-long reading I found that three-fourths of the critical materials said one or more of the following:

1. Meaning is undecidable.
2. Literary texts are entangled in discourses of race, class and gender.
3. Some concept or the other is a cultural construct.

As we know, the first is a theoretical insight of deconstruction. The second comes to us from schools of ideological criticism, such as postcolonialism, Marxism and feminism. Harold Bloom terms these collectively 'the School of Resentment' (1995, 23). The third demonstrates constructivism, the 'in-thing' in academia today. Gender is a construct. So is sexuality, nation, subject, disability and what not. Heck! Literature itself is a construct. Later I learnt that these tendencies were representative of contemporary literary criticism in general. I also learnt that statements that did not say any of these three things were likely to be dismissed as 'humanistic'.

Without doubt, without irony, it may be conceded that each of the above-mentioned tendencies – textual deconstruction, ideological criticism and constructivism – deserves the tag of Copernican revolutions in literary studies. They have helped us look at texts, language and the world itself, in unprecedented ways. Their legacy to humanistic disciplines in general, and to literary studies and cultural theory in particular, may be discerned from the drastic changes evident in the orientation and methodology of these disciplines in the last fifty years. The purpose of the following sections is not to question the validity of these approaches but to understand their implications. In short, our discussion here does not belong to the field of objections to theory. True, theory is a much-maligned entity; a lot of theory is dismissed as 'high funda' stuff, as abstruse, self-perpetuating rhetoric. But the point is *not* that theory is fetishized. That is tantamount to a belated attempt to inaugurate the post-phase of just another critical cult (fad, if you like!). The response here is directed at the unselfconscious application of these theoretical frameworks to more and more texts the way a game is played with changing players. Are future literary criticism and literary research destined to be an aggregate of these games: the undecidability-game, the (counter-)ideology-game and the constructivist-game? To harness the possibilities beyond these 'trite games', one has to examine the function of theory in actual research.

3.2 The Return of Deductive Reasoning

As we know, a theory is a system of generalized explanations, used as a framework to understand a phenomenon. In the sciences, a theory also serves the function of predicting and controlling the phenomenon in question. In literary studies, theories help understand and interpret a text, an author, a genre or an epoch. But what exactly is the nature of the relation between the object of study (the text/the author/the genre/the epoch) and the theoretical framework in actual research? What do frames do to facts? Do frames colour the facts in question? More often than not, research begins with certain a priori assumptions – a grid – and the final product becomes a mere application of these assumptions to a few more texts. In this kind of 'school-research', one can predict the findings of three to five years of research from the initial proposal itself. Then, what is singular about each research enterprise is simply the evidence culled from the text to prove the a priori thesis. One gets a sense that this is return of 'deductive (syllogistic) reasoning' in another form: All humans are mortal; Socrates is human; so he is mortal. Likewise, gender is a construct; so is sexuality, subject and literature itself. It is this construct that we generally find in literary works. We find it in work x (x = *The Mahabharata, The Aeneid, The Canterbury Tales, As You Like It, Pride and Prejudice, Middlemarch, Women in Love*, etc.). Moreover, the texts themselves are part of the discursive processes which produce these constructs.

Replication of theoretical assumptions with regard to more and more texts might not be plagiarism, but if it is research, it is a passive exercise of intellect, it is repetitive – it is a formula. If application of theory is a passive intellectual exercise and renders research sterile, as is often the case, can we, then, abandon theoretical frameworks altogether? To use a provisional metaphor, can a text come out of the theoretical cloud? This is not a rhetorical question, though it has the ring of one. Therefore, it is imperative to be attentive to the subtleties of the distinctions we make rather than be contented with the general thrust of our claims and arguments. Let us assume for a while that theoretical readings of texts are *extrinsic* literary criticism. If theoretical readings of texts are extrinsic criticism, is there an *intrinsic* criticism, which is antithetical to the former? Are there objectively existing facts in a literary text that come with their own interpretation? As the American philosopher Thomas Nagel famously put it, 'facts need frames'. Nagel's book is significantly entitled *The View from Nowhere* (1986). One may suspend one's 'interests' while reflecting on a phenomenon or object in a temporarily detached mode of interaction, but pertinently, there is no view from nowhere. Every view is obtained from a perspective. Every interpretation is made from a particular point of view. To discover what purportedly lies beyond theory, we have to ascertain the exact nature of the relation between the theoretical framework and the object of study.

3.3 Facts and Frames

The encounter between the knowing subject and the object known, or to be known, has been the chief concern, and one of the perennial fascinations, of epistemology. René Descartes, with whom modern philosophy is widely believed to have emerged, viewed it as a detached and disinterested relation between an autonomous subject and the object which is out there in the world. Martin Heidegger, in his philosophical magnum opus *Being and Time* (*Sein und Zeit*), contested the idea of interpretation (*Auslegung*) as the encounter of a detached and disinterested (Cartesian) subject with an object. To Heidegger (1962), interpretation was ontologically grounded in prior structures of understanding (*Vorstruktur*, translated into English as 'fore-structure'). These structures are a function of 'being-in-the-world', of *Dasein*'s having projected himself *there* (*Dasein* literally means both 'being there' and 'Being itself'). There is no ground zero for approaching knowledge. The knowing subject is conditioned prior to the encounter with the object of knowledge. This is no inherent epistemic disability but one of the conditions to be factored in, in understanding the dynamics of knowledge. In fact, the (meta-) knowledge of epistemic structures has been a liberating development in the history of ideas. For instance, Gayatri Chakravorty Spivak's concept of 'epistemic violence' (1988, 280) in the essay 'Can the Subaltern Speak?' is premised on the idea that the norms of discourse among the First World intellectuals render it difficult to understand the cultural subtleties of practices and problems in the so-called Third World. As said earlier, knowledge in the humanities, as opposed to that of 'hard science', is known for its broader subjective and cultural bases. Understanding this helps in two ways. First, it enables the philosopher of knowledge to be on guard against epistemic outrages of the sort articulated by Spivak. Second, it gives her/him access to modalities of diligent reasoning which generates 'valid' knowledge.

The 'perspectival' conditioning of the subject is not the only factor which problematizes the epistemic endeavour. Characteristics innate to the object render even preliminary attempts at knowledge a process which is complex but worthy of understanding. The object is multidimensional. One cannot perceive or understand all the aspects of the object, at least all at once.[1] Change of metaphor – facet, dimension, part, side or feature – does not help here; language is fundamentally metaphorical, and even while dealing with non-physical entities it is compelled to rely on the physicality of the physical world for its metaphorical extensions of reference. Quotidian experience teaches us that one cannot apprehend all the dimensions of a physical object. Probably, there *is* such a thing as what Immanuel Kant called the *Ding an sich* (the thing in itself), but the access to it can only be mediated. Our perceptual apparatus has its limitations. But our cognitive apparatus, aspiring though it may be, with a broader field to grapple with, is even more limited. This is so not only because cognition is conditioned and 'biased' as stated earlier but also because thoughts, beyond our calculations, interact and create links, even remote ones, which bear on the understanding of the object under consideration. Our discussion here, particularly when it takes up cognition, operates in an area which is beyond Kantian 'categories', which are more about the 'basic' processes of perception and understanding.[2] Selectivity vis-à-vis the features of the object is one of the organizing principles of cognition, analogous to the principles of perception.[3]

If a theory is a set of concepts and assumptions which provides a scaffold to understand and explain the phenomenon under study (here, a text), do we have something like intrinsic concepts, that is, concepts which emerge from within the text? Do texts have models and paradigms that are innate to them? Philosophically speaking, multidimensionality of the object (the text) and the perspectival conditioning of the subject (the reader/critic) vis-à-vis the object have rendered selectivity of perception inevitable. Therefore, with some qualifications, one can concede that there is no intrinsic criticism as such. We see what we look for in a text. We need to know what we have to look for. The text, like the world, demands concepts and categories not only to understand it but also to decide what we want to understand. In this sense, a framework is indispensable to the task of interpreting a text. But every concept is a potential framework, with the capacity to coalesce with related concepts to form a full-fledged interpretive framework. A theoretical framework is a conceptual *system*. And textual 'invitation' to concepts is direct in some cases. In other words, some concepts and frameworks are more appropriate than others to the interpretation of particular textual data. Criticism is invocation of a concept at the back of our minds in relation to a text. Who would have thought that chaos theory would one day be brought in to interpret literary texts (I have in mind Peter Francis Mackey's book *Chaos Theory and James Joyce's Everyman*)?[4] The texts themselves may add to the reader-critic's repertoire of concepts. Although from a relativistic point of view it may be fashionable to concede that there is no intrinsic criticism as such, texts, in the above sense, can throw up ways of dealing with them. This is because concepts are neither within nor without texts. Concepts emerge from experience, but an endeavour to 'locate' them would be a belated Platonic wild-goose chase – a conundrum past its age of interest.

The seductive aspect of the three popular theoretical frameworks mentioned earlier – textual deconstruction, ideological criticism and constructivism – is that they apply to the world, language and literature in general. They are totalizing in their scope. In their vulgar versions, they allow critics merely to 'match' their a priori assumptions and concepts with 'suitable' textual data but exclude the possibility of additional, unorthodox, extra-scholastic (non-school) insights from emerging. This is logically possible regardless of whether the textual world is singular or not.

3.4 The Enterprise of Ideological Criticism

We will be looking at the question of ideology of literature more than once in the course of our discussion. (The final chapter is devoted to the relation between the aesthetic and the political.) To begin with, ideological criticism is a sub-type of what Paul Ricoeur terms the 'hermeneutics of suspicion' (1981, 34). According to Ricoeur, hermeneutics of suspicion is a mode of interpretation which aims to reveal disguised meanings: 'This type of hermeneutics is animated by [...] a skepticism towards the given, and it is characterized by a distrust of the symbol as a dissimulation of the real' (6). Ricoeur contrasts this kind of hermeneutics with the 'hermeneutics of faith', concerned with the 'restoration' of meanings. He designates the demythologizers of modernity – Marx, Nietzsche and Freud – 'masters of suspicion', who 'look upon the contents of consciousness as in some sense 'false'; all three aim to transcend this falsity through a reductive interpretation and critique' (6). Ideological criticism is a necessary but insufficient phase of criticism. No doubt, as history amply demonstrates, to be conscious of ideology is a prerequisite for freedom: a 'hermeneutic of suspicion' is essential to a hermeneutic of possibilities. In practical criticism, ideological consciousness has contributed to the inclusion of politically excluded possibilities. Is this the only reason why ideological criticism has been so sexy? This is one enterprise in which critical intelligence is directly polemical and antagonistic. In an age of spectacle and sensation, only extremes catch our attention, and extreme articulations have a mnemonic value in retrospect. Extreme forms of ideological criticism implicitly believe that it is quite naïve even to think of a non-ideological perspective, patriarchal to be even willing to consider any concept other than gender, quite bourgeois to welcome any factor other than class, quite precolonial to think anything other than race, subjugation and epistemic/cultural violence.

Why are certain theoretical approaches particularly appealing? One may account for this popularity in terms of the uncanny, and often unrecognized connections between the experiential and the theoretical, between the academic world and the 'real' world – that of everyday life. Behind the human decision to 'cathect' a particular idea or theory is what may be termed *a penchant for embeddedness*, the desire or need to see one's experience as part of a larger framework, phenomenon or ensemble. Our cathexis of ideas – that is, our psychic investment in them – has a prehistory. We respond to those ideas which experientially make sense on the cognitive-affective continuum. Ideological criticism deals with issues whose connections to the non-academic terrain – developments in the larger world – are clearer than in the case of other paradigms. Since its connections to the life outside academia are close and discernible, ideological criticism appears as a socially relevant intellectual endeavour. It is easier to see the parallels between the networks of power discovered by Edward Said in his 'contrapuntal reading' (1994, 36, 59) of *Jane Eyre* and *Mansfield Park*, and multinational corporations depriving ordinary people of drinking water and clean air, big dams displacing people and the land wars in various parts of the world. A straight analogy is assumed among the colonial, the neocolonial (neoliberal, if you like) and the statist. For this reason ideological critiques seem more 'natural' than application of a framework such as chaos theory. It satisfies the criterion of social relevance with cognitive ease. Remember Susan Fiske's and Shelley Taylor's theory of social cognition – the human mind is a cognitive miser. Ideological criticism is a critical endeavour which affords cognitive ease in quite a few ways. It is based on a simple binaristic model: You are either subversive or complicit, naïve or critical, gullible or suspicious. More often than not, suspicion is valid. We live in an age of proxy-discourses. Most nefarious objectives can be clandestinely pursued in the name of the most acceptable ideals.

Further, the popularity of the power-and-ideology paradigm lies in its totalizing articulation. Power and ideology are ubiquitous. From this perspective of Hegelian-Marxist holism, ideology is the very structure of everything. Subjects are constituted in ideology. Ideology naturalizes the status quo. It decides the terms of discourse and constitutes the matrix of our thoughts. The third reason for its appeal is the assertion concerning the implicit character of ideology; even the most neutral of human practices are deeply ideological, but one is not aware of this. Ideological criticism also has an element of concealed elitism. Whom does it actually empower? For those who have been at the receiving end of adverse power relations and ideological manipulation (e.g., the Dalits, or those who occupy the lower rungs of caste hierarchy in India), power and ideology are genuine, existential issues. As for others, the approach appeals to their self-concept and offers narcissistic contrasts. Ideological criticism envisages an in-group, an intellectually elite group which is 'critical' (read 'suspicious enough'). Behind the naiveté-suspicion paradigm is the assumption that the critical elite has transcended susceptibility to ideological naiveté, through specialized training or through 'close reading', but the rest of the world has not. We are critical; the other readers are naïve. We have the theoretical repertoire; they have not. We have an insight into the real nature of world's processes, they have not. This approach also appeals to the altruistic aspects of our self. It gives us the illusory satisfaction of being like benevolent feudal lords, romantically ruined as the Irish landlords were in the course of their attempts to help the tenants during the nineteenth-century potato famine. Here is an intellectual elitism that purports to contest social elitism but which actually replicates the latter. To sum up, ideological criticism affords the consolation of a personally and socially satisfactory way of using the intellect. It contextualizes intellect; it factors in the world; it is more socioculturally holistic. It is progressively (or patronizingly) elitist. It offers cognitive ease. Besides, it offers belated rhetorical compensations for old naiveté, for a wasted time of 'reading for pleasure', when we were blissfully unaware of ideology in the text!

A major addition to the concept of ideology, which is important for our discussion, has been made by Louis Althusser (1971) – the 'interpellation' of the subject. Althusser's focus in this regard is the need of capitalism to produce the kind of people for its continuance. The modern capitalist state produces its productive workers through two types of institutions: Repressive State Apparatuses (police, army, law courts, etc.) and Ideological State Apparatuses (the Church, the family, political parties, the media and the educational system). The Repressive State Apparatuses function 'by violence'; by contrast, the Ideological State Apparatuses function 'by ideology'. Ideology 'hail[s]' concrete individuals and fits them into a particular role and pre-fixed 'subject-position' through a process called 'interpellation'. According to Althusser, if individuals experience themselves as autonomous subjects, it is the result of ideology. To insist on Althusser's insistence, it *is* ideology. Ideology 'exists by constituting concrete subjects as subjects [...] The existence of ideology and the hailing or interpellation of individuals as subjects are one and the same thing' (1971, 173, 175). It is this notion of the objectified non-subject which Althusser's disciple, Michel Foucault, has popularized for contemporary cultural theory. According to Foucault, institutions and practices (he calls the ensemble of statements produced by these 'discourse') produce socially integrated subjects. In order to address fascism in the head, the critique of ideology should be directed at ourselves. This is the dilemma of a subject – let us use the term provisionally – who is constituted and has an existence only in discourse, and hence, many theorists maintain, cannot critique it from its implicated position.

To give up the possibility of a meta-position, which actually exists, is to succumb to what may be called *cultural fatalism*. Are we really ideological pawns? Even as we are constituted as subjects by and in ideology, we retain the capacity for 'metacognition'. We are capable of thinking about our thinking sequentially though not simultaneously. We can ask ourselves: Why do I hold this view?' and 'What are the assumptions that lie behind my actions? There may not be a neurological distinction between a thought and a metathought, but there is a philosophical one. If no meta-position is possible, how can an ideological critic do what others do not? Further, the subject is not a static entity. S/he is in perpetual change. S/he draws upon, manipulates and recreates herself/himself out of the repertoire of the quotidian – the multiplicity of its discourses and possible practices. We use concepts and values from one discourse/practice to understand and critique concepts and values of another discourse/practice, in order to have a nuanced and critical understanding of the world. At least in part, the autonomy of the subject is that of the *bricoleur*.

Literally, the word *bricoleur* means a tinker, but by extension, it suggests one who is capable of making creative use of what is available. Texts are part of the bricoleur-subject's (re-)creative exercises.

3.5 Constructivism

The idea that a concept was a historical/cultural/discursive construct was floated to contest and challenge entrenched essentialist notions surrounding them. Though in retrospect it might seem implausible, for a long period of time in history, people believed that to be a woman was to be submissive, passive, irrational and emotional. In many quarters, to be able to see some concept as a construct is considered a paradigm shift necessary for freedom and emancipation; and it is true. This recognition concerning the true nature of a concept opens it to critique and reformulation. As Richard Rorty puts it, it is 'the sense that there is nothing deep down inside us except what we have put there ourselves, no criterion that we have not created in the course of creating a practice' (1982, xviii). Today we know the constructed character of truth, subject, gender, sexuality, nation, disability and what not. Any position other than this is liberal humanistic or essentialist fallacy. Eagleton, however, points to the flipside of this position: 'One advantage of the dogma that we are the prisoners of our own discourse, unable to advance reasonably certain truth-claims because such claims are merely relative to our language, is that it allows you to drive a coach and horses through everybody else's beliefs while not saddling you with the inconvenience of having to adopt any yourself' (1996, 125). The genius of humanism, however diligent, is easily rebuked by the deconstructive angel as Mark Antony's was by Caesar's.

The root question here is: Do concepts emerge from historical experience? Or, do they have an ahistorical existence and character? We intuitively know that concepts are product of historical experience. A position to the contrary is a Platonic vestige – a belated hold out – more an exception than a rule in the postmodern world. The tendency to pretend otherwise stems from a desire to see the rest of the world conceptually backward, an analogue of the concealed elitism of ideological criticism. But our focus here is on the logical implications of constructivism, not its (quasi-Nietzschean) psychological genesis. Like pan-ideologism, constructivism is totalizing and another version of the naiveté-suspicion paradigm. Once you posit that all reality is discursive, how do you even attempt to prove the contrary? The endeavour would be similar to the Realist/Idealist epistemological question. Does the world really exist, or is it a creation of our senses? Is the world exactly as we perceive through our senses, or is it merely a version produced by the senses? How does one answer this question? We have not known the world without the senses! The only proof to the contrary is that many people perceive the world this way. If you transposed this answer to the field of concepts, the retort would be that we are all made in discourse. Experience, which might have been a method to verify, has been distrusted as discursively mediated. Entities might have an experiential meaning, where there are no conceptual meanings, though. If to show that something has an essential reality is humanistic naiveté, to show the contrary is a logical impossibility. A counter-hypothesis is logically ruled out. And that is the end of reasoning. It gives the comfort of a meta-position while denying the possibility of such a position. Indeed a disarming strategy!

For sure, conceptions change over time, from culture to culture and even from person to person. When one is told that a text reveals some concept to be a construct, all that one needs to say is: 'Whether x is a construct or not depends on the nature and history of x'. 'How can you say that Homer was disabled? – Ancient Greeks did not have the concept of disability!' The response to the question is: 'If the ancient Greeks did not have the concept, why did the Spartans throw deformed children from the hilltop in the interest of a eugenically perfect state?' The Greek conception of disability was possibly different from ours. Whether the Greeks had a conception of disability or not is a matter of historical research, not answerable by the readymade formula that everything is discursive. The problem is that reality has been transposed exclusively on to the level of discourse, to rhetorical contexts. We have decided not to go beyond the level of 'naming'.

Let us also pose in this context the question as to whether constructivism, and its corollary, relativism, are desirable per se. How fruitful is the venture of problematizing the referent? The utility of the exercise depends upon what is at stake and upon whose merchandise we are selling. Are human rights a Western construct, a stick used to beat China or other authoritarian regimes? If so, can we begin neglecting the concept of human rights in law, in everyday life and in academia? Let me illustrate the problem with the concept of the human and the humanist discourse. The chief problem with prescriptive definitions of the human is that those who do not conform to the projected ideal – originally, *homo humanus* was the antithesis of *homo barbarus* – are deemed the undesirable other who have to be 'civilized', or retained for contrastive self-definitions or to be even done away with. The first two tendencies were evident in the 'white-man's-burden' narrative of European cultural imperialism, the classical and Christian arguments in favour of slavery, the policy of white Australia, South African apartheid regimes and contemporary visa restrictions in the Western world. The whole colonial enterprise was premised on the idea of Western civilization as the beacon light of enlightened humanity. According to the postcolonial counter-narrative, universal man is a partisan construct whose other is a savage in the dialectic of self-construction. The third is assumed in the surprisingly legitimized warrants for extermination of the Jews, the Roma and Sinti and the homosexuals in Nazi Germany – *Untermenschen* (subhuman; literally, *Untermensch* means underman). Those who do not fulfil the unwritten criteria are perceived as a threat to the envisaged utopia and are either subordinated or annihilated, a tendency which was executed with apocalyptic urgency by the Nazis. Every ideal requires an 'other' for its opposite. The nonideal is projected on to the other. For this reason, every brand of humanism that fastidiously insists of 'applicants' to the (culturally defined) human status on showing a 'grade card' is innately dubious.

But the human can never be confined to a discourse of qualification. While deconstructive challenges to the notion of the human do have an emancipative 'humanist' function, their validity depends upon the nature of the other discourses upon which these challenges have a bearing – whether it is a *discourse of rights* or a *discourse of qualification* – and upon the question what precisely is *at stake*? A cause of misunderstandings in the humanist/anti-humanist debates has been the confusion between the two discourses. In order to clear the air, one has to examine in what discourse the concept of the human figures. If what is at stake is something of as high a value as the right to life, freedom, dignity or justice, conceptual nitpicking is redundant and counterproductive. Here we have humanism as an understatement of causes. Where the stakes are high – custodial deaths, executions without the due process of law, fake encounters, various forms of child abuse and social discrimination – constructivist truisms do not suffice.[5] That is also why many reified definitions of man, more disabling than enabling, have been most detrimental to the humanist cause. It is more or less recognized today that what we need is a humanism that allows for plural, complex and fluid criteria. When it comes to the question of rights, the human must have the loosest definitions and the broadest bases and embrace the most diverse conditions. It is due to this need for the broadest base that several humanisms (often without named so) have adopted criteria by which the last in the social order benefit, John Ruskin's 'Unto this Last' and the Antyodaya movement in India being obvious examples.

As the foregoing discussion illustrates, the discourse of rights places a non-negotiable value on the category of the human though the conceptual content be negotiable. That the concept was arbitrarily defined in the past does not warrant rendering the category impotent or getting rid of it altogether, which is tantamount to throwing the baby out with the bathwater. The battle of human causes cannot be fought on any other ground lest we risk endless fragmentation on lines of race, class, ethnicity, gender and so on. As Martin Halliwell and Mousley point out, 'An ethically and politically grounded humanism is necessary to know when he or she is being degraded and what human agency is when it is denied' (2003, 2). It is conceded that 'the human', despite its inherent limitations, uncanny impersonality and historical appropriations, needs to be retained as a benchmarking category to indicate degradation and dehumanisation. To be effective, a benchmark has to be as precise as possible. For this reason, Halliwell and Mousley are sceptical about 'too much openness [and endless nitpicking in defining the human, which] may lead to a complete loss of the human':

> One reason for a grounded humanism is that if the human does not operate as some kind of given, then words like alienation, depersonalization and degradation lose their evaluative value and ethical force [...] it is surely necessary to have some sense of what human is when he or she is being degraded [...] the notion of endless plasticity and pliability of the human. [...] is tantamount to suggesting that human beings can live under any conditions whatsoever. (10)

One may find a parallel to this need for the human constant in the postcolonial/feminist retention of a 'strategic essentialism' (Gayatri Chakravorty Spivak's coinage; also a term used by Margaret Whitford and Naomi Schor to describe Luce Irigaray's position), lest the struggles waged on behalf of the subaltern or in the name of women's causes lose their anchor.

What is celebrated by anti-foundationalist thinkers (e.g., Michel Foucault) is the death of a concept in its sacrosanct avatar. As such, the demise of man portends his new incarnation. According to Halliwell and Mousley, 'Like Nietzsche, who saw the "death of God" as the unprecedented opportunity for the individual to surpass him or herself, Foucault sees this moment as the liberation from "man" as fixed essence, as the anchor of knowledge and as transcendental ideal' (2003, 164). Since every past conceptualization of 'the human' and of humanism was historically and culturally specific and had a subtext of incompleteness, the only way in which the enterprise of humanism could sustain itself was in the form of a temporally evolving idea through open-ended, pluralistic, participative, dialogical and self-conscious expansion of the discourse across previously excluded spaces, groups and cultures. In other words, the impossibility of a transhistorical type to demonstrate the realization of human potential – the gap between historical articulation and conceptual possibility – rendered contestation inevitable. The humanist project is aware of this gap; self-critique and self-reflexivity are germane to it. In fact, humanism's capacity for self-critique has been its greatest strength.[6] The humanist discourse has indeed internally heterogenized, factoring in differences and claims of race, class, gender and sexuality. A non-teleological forward movement (i.e., without a pre-fixed *telos*, or goal) is the present trend.

The mistake of the past was to take a fragment for the whole picture. More importantly, the picture can be completed only futuristically. To borrow a metaphor from Roland Barthes (1977), the human is both 'a work' that is historically bound and 'a text' which fulfils only in its destination. The conceptual possibilities of the human are so unpredictable at any particular moment in history that one can think of only a futuristic consummation. Under the temporally emended paradigm, it can be seen that the conceptual evolution of the human will continue till the end of human history and of humanity's intellectual engagements.

To sum up, constructivism is not necessarily emancipative in that it reduces different truth-claims, and truths with different stakes, to the same level. Therefore, there is good reason to suspect that it will not automatically enthrone formerly marginalized populations and recognize previously excluded realities. One can brand something undecidable and discursive if it is experientially negotiable. And there are experiential realities which no amount of relativism can salvage, save or reject. The lived reality called life is too high a value to allow relativism. It is beyond plausibility to believe that the inmates of the Nazi concentration camps who were fortunate enough to be liberated, or victims of social discrimination, will concur with the formula that their lived reality is a discursive construct, or that all they have is their own or the others' narrative representations of the same.

3.6 *Ce qui arrive (réellement)*: What Does Deconstruction Actually 'Mean'?

Not surprisingly, introductions and companions to, and commentaries on, Jacques Derrida/deconstruction, true to their subject matter, are unusually self-reflexive and self-conscious, if not narcissistic, and take a *via negativa* (the analogue with Apophatic theology lightheartedly indicates an impossibility in defining deconstruction akin to that of defining God!) in attempting to fulfil the task of exposition. By contagion, they also showcase paradoxes and contradictions, and have an understandable overdose of caveats. This is due perhaps to the understanding that deconstruction is, with its ingrained self-applicability, conceptually singular, to use the adjectival form of one of Derrida's favourite words – *singularity*. Derrida himself made the self-applicability of deconstruction clear when he asserted that 'we cannot utter a single deconstructive proposition which has not already slipped into the form, the logic and the implicit postulations of precisely what it seeks to contest' (1972, 250). An endeavour to define deconstruction is said to be a semantic contradiction and goes against the very (anti-foundationalist) spirit of what the term tends to signify – a philosophical position, a concept, a school, a literary theory, a critical practice, a method of reading or whatever it seeks to 'pin down'. According to Derrida, 'Prefaces, along with forewords, introductions, preludes, preliminaries, preambles, prologues and prolegomena, have always been written, it seems, in view of their own self-effacement' (1981, 7). As for his own definitions (or strategic non-definitions), Derrida says in 'The Time is Out of Joint': 'I have often had occasion to define deconstruction as that which is – far from a theory, a school, a method, even a discourse, still less a technique that can be appropriated – at bottom *what happens or comes to pass* [*ce qui arrive*]' (1995, 17; emphasis as in the source). The crux of what actually happens – *ce qui arrive* – with deconstruction is mired in the cautionary elusiveness and self-reflexive illustrations of elucidatory enterprises and labyrinthine cautionary tales, probably triggered by Derrida's own enigmatic, quasi-cryptic writing and contestations of 'conventional semantic values' (Wolfreys 1998, 3). These tendencies, more often than not, deprive the reader of a handle on the object under consideration. One may, however, for heuristic purposes, go against the caveats and cautions, and find a point of departure in one, if not the chief, of the principles of deconstruction – *a conceptual negotiability innate to any discourse*, or *a tension intrinsic to the concept* (or conceptual constants which Derrida calls *philosophemes*) *itself*. Derrida's examples for intra-conceptual tension popularly include 'the center' and 'the gift'.

Let us recall the conceptual schema about concepts which was elucidated in Chapter 2. The vocabulary of a language consists of a hierarchy of concepts. On the top of the hierarchy are macro-concepts (e.g., the concept of life, declared a humanist abstraction in the post-structuralist critical climate). These are generalized ideas whose particular manifestations are expressed using micro-concepts (e.g., a life of suffering). These micro-concepts are macro-concepts to concepts which are still lower in the hierarchy. The answer to the question 'What kind of suffering?' (e.g., poverty, starvation, confinement, torture or destitution) is the corresponding micro-concept to the macro-concept immediately above in the hierarchy. The lower one moves down the hierarchy, the more particular the reference becomes. Particular meanings, or ideas, recalled by the mind, are particularized ramifications or instantiations of the concepts. When one looks from the top of the hierarchy, one can see only abstractions. This is inevitable as these are abstracted from concrete, particular instances of what the concept signifies in experience. The macro-concept bears only an inadequate 'trace' of the particular experience. When one speaks of a macro-concept, the micro-concepts that are invoked have among them only what Ludwig Wittgenstein might have called a 'family resemblance' (*Familienähnlichkeit*). *Différance* and the 'play' (*jeu*) of signifiers are a story of such conceptual ramifications – ramifications that destabilize any putative generality.

The above narrative of deconstruction entails much. On the one hand, deconstruction has revealed an unsettling feature of language by which every statement is infused with an in-built instability, undecidability and alogicality which compromises its truth-claims. Derrida has indeed driven a wedge of alogicality (or, logic of illogicality) into the Western philosophical tradition. His philosophical legacy, though it spans several disciplines and objects of study, rests primarily on his critique of *logocentrism* – 'metaphysics of presence' – which, to him, characterizes most of Western philosophical thought. The Johannine Gospel, written for a Greek audience, might serve as a point of reference for Derrida's own Judaeo-Greek intellectual pedigree. The Gospel famously opens as follows: 'In the beginning was the Word, and the Word was with God, and the Word was God'. The Greek word for the Word is *Logos*. St John used it to establish the pre-existence of the Son in the Holy Trinity before Jesus's earthly mission:

> As a designation of Christ, therefore, *Logos* is peculiarly felicitous because, (1) in Him are embodied all the treasures of the divine wisdom, the collective 'thought' of God. [...]; and, (2) He is, from eternity, but especially in His incarnation, the utterance or expression of the Person, and 'thought' of deity [...] In the Being, Person, and work of Christ Deity is told out. (Notes to the passage in the Scofield Reference Bible)

Greek *Logos* means a variety of things: word, speech, knowledge, wisdom, thought, governing reason, organizing principle and so on. Above all, in the Biblical sense, it signifies: (1) a thought or concept; and (2) the expression or utterance of thought. The word itself suggests an identity of thought/concept and the utterance of the thought, which guarantees a stable meaning. Derrida reveals a rupture between the two. His inversion and de-binarization of speech/writing as well as its near-replacement with the idea of 'contamination' by the 'other' ('nonsynonymous substitutions'; Derrida 1991, 65) flows from such ruptured identities. Every thought, idea or concept is contaminated by other thoughts, ideas and concepts. That the signifier and the signified have only a gliding relationship – 'chance meetings' (Wolfreys 1998, 103) – has always been a feature of language and a condition of writing.

On the other hand, rather than articulating a 'weakness' in language, deconstruction celebrates its unlimited onto-semantic potential. The text renews itself across spaces and ages due to its 'textuality'. Many 'worlds' (even futuristic ones) are implicit in language, which are invoked when the reader meets the signifiers on the page. The 'black marks on a page' are capable of invoking many worlds. *Iterability*, Derrida's polyglottal portmanteau term, describes the capacity of signs and texts to be repeated in new situations and to produce new meanings (1982) in their 'transactions'. The term encapsulates Sanskrit *itera* (other) and Latin *iterare* (to repeat). For an instance of *iterability*, upon first reading the Biblical passage 'For unto every one that hath shall be given, and he shall have abundance: but from him that hath not shall be taken away even that which he hath' (Matthew 25: 29), I, born in a Syrian Christian household in the left bastion of Kerala, thought, particularly in the light of the popular characterization of Jesus Christ as the first socialist, that it was a critique of acquisitive society and of the socio-economic condition in which the rich got richer and the poor, poorer. Educational psychology may find in the passage a metaphor for the additive character of learning. A passage signifies differently because of the relatability of the words to multiple contexts, with different implications for different life-worlds. This potential of language lies at the core of all possibilities of cross-cultural concretization of texts. In other words, deconstruction affirms the capacity of language for creating unanticipated symmetries with auctorially unforeseen experiential worlds. Of course, whether signs without human intention constitute language at all is debatable – a question that pertains to the ontology of language. For instance, for Stephen Knapp and Walter Benn Michaels, this is only a semblance of language (1982, 728).

That deconstruction is not mere literary theory is implied in the elusiveness of the elucidatory endeavours alluded to at the beginning of this section. In a sense, the history of literary theory is itself a narrative of changing relationships among four entities – language, text, the self and the world. Two key tendencies of twentieth-century theory – linguistic/textual deconstruction and ideology-critique – take off from two insights articulated by Friedrich Nietzsche. If Derrida is heir to the former, Foucault is one of the several intellectual descendants of the latter. The 'linguistic turn' can probably be traced back to Nietzsche's well-known statement on the metaphoricity of truth in *On Truth and Lies in a Nonmoral Sense* (1873):

> What then is truth? A mobile army of metaphors, metonymies, anthropomorphisms – in short, a sum of human relations which, poetically and rhetorically intensified, became transposed and adorned, and which after long usage by a people seem fixed, canonical and binding on them. Truths are illusions which one has forgotten *are* illusions, worn-out metaphors which have become powerless to affect the sense. (Nietzsche 1973, 46; italics as in the source)

Derrida echoes Nietzsche when he discusses the figures of 'the structure' and 'the center': 'The history of metaphysics [...] is the history of these metaphors and metonymies';[7] and Heidegger in the following sentence: 'Its matrix [...] is the determination of Being as presence in all senses of the word' (Derrida

1978, 279). The fixation – institutional, linguistic, philosophical and cultural – that Nietzsche mentions is the target of deconstruction, which reveals it to be the subject of lexico-conceptual *jeu*. Elsewhere, Nietzsche demonstrates how apparently neutral and rational concepts such as truth and morality were originally matters of political expediency, ruses contrived to serve the interests of particular groups. For instance, in *On the Genealogy of Morals* (1887) he showed how Judaeo-Christian ennoblement of values of meekness, humility, poverty, suffering and piety was a craftily sublimated expression of slaves' *ressentiment* (often translated as 'resentment') against, and ideological revenge upon, their masters. The suspicion of much contemporary theory and criticism is directed, quite legitimately, at concealed ideologies. We shall briefly discuss the relationship between deconstruction and contestation of ideologies a little later.

3.6.1 The auto-epiphany of Western thought

In any case, deconstruction occupies a pertinent place in the history of the Occident's attempts at world-conceptualization. The world process is intricate, complex, multistranded, tantalizingly unwieldy and often inscrutable. As I have argued in Chapter 1, for reasons of cognitive economy, the temptation to make sense of the process using 'single-entity tropes' has been quite strong in intellectual history. Ancient religion provided the earliest trope in the form of deities. This propensity extends to modern concepts as diverse as Friedrich Hegel's Absolute Spirit, whose 'outworking' or unfolding is the progress of both consciousness and human history; Arthur Schopenhauer's Will (all striving); Henri Bergson's *élan vital* (vital impetus); Oswald Spengler's inner historical directionality of cultures; and Charles Darwin's natural selection, albeit with limited explanatory ambitions. One of the tendencies in this history has been the self-reflexive turn to the human subject, mental principles (à la Immanuel Kant) and cultural, linguistic and representational schemata as the ground of world-theorization. Now where does deconstruction stand in this long history? Derrida and deconstruction may be argued as representing a climactic problematization of this history of world-theorizations. We shall briefly explore how. What language captures is only an abstract, limited in multiple senses, of the world process (the world in its broadest conceptions and in the largest ontological sense). The abstract is haunted by what it cannot capture, foresee or limit, by the proliferent *excess* of the world process, plurality of experience, shiftability of modes of being, the intricacies of many a *Lebenswelt* and the world's extensive anastomosis in time, space and consciousness. If we reckon only the word, we can see only the 'differential fraying' in language. But what is of greater significance is the fact that deconstruction reveals the gaping gulf that opens between *world-conceptualization* (in language) and *world-excess* – an assertion of the latter against a whole self-assured history of the former. This 'hauntological' inevitability, whether acknowledged or not, is the *auto-epiphany* (if not an anti-epiphany) of Western thought, and, in this sense, deconstruction may be classed in the same category, though they belong to different domains of knowledge and despite internal differences, as Thomas Kuhn's 'paradigm shift', Werner Heisenberg's 'uncertainty principle' and Albert Einstein's 'theory of relativity'.

3.6.2 'Put a pin in that chap, will you?': Deconstruction in critical practice

To the philosopher's objection (à la Rodolphe Gasché's[8]) that literary-critical use of deconstruction is not philosophical enough, the critic may respond by pointing out, rightly or otherwise, that what deconstruction seeks to identify in discourse – conceptual negotiability and/or intra-conceptual tension – has always been there. When ancient deconstructive thought as old as *pharmakon* (remedy, poison and scapegoat) reaches Derrida post a Heideggerian detour of fundamental ontology (Being in itself – *das Sein* as opposed to *das Seiende* – precursor to the critique of 'presence') and several other unimmediate antecedents, what makes the movement momentous, at least to the literary critic, is the new reading – something which prompts J. Hillis Miller to describe deconstruction as 'nothing more or less than good reading as such' (1987, 10), or rhetorical analysis of literary texts. Is deconstruction just another kind of 'good' reading? Is it like any other method of reading, like say feminist, Marxist, psychoanalytic and postcolonial ones. To be sure, each of them destabilizes a hermeneutic ground. It is easy to categorize Derrida alongside the other 'masters of suspicion' whom Ricoeur lists. Derrida re-examines the fundamentals of thought, language, conceptualization, writing and reading, and breaks up the critical ground which was for long taken for granted. But can language as ground be considered on par with patriarchy, reason, truth, consciousness and epistemes? Perhaps feminist, Marxist, psychoanalytic and postcolonial criticisms can be deemed deconstructions of the respective discourses they contest. But Derridean interrogations, far from the exclusive impression their technicization conveys, plough the very ground of all knowledge and discourse, and involve a meta-engagement. Small wonder it has served as the conceptual fount, and perhaps a natural ally, of all critical contestations, despite the charge of it being ahistorical and apolitical. This charge, however, deserves attention. For instance, according to John M. Ellis,

> Feminists and Marxists are very mistaken to see support for their position in deconstruction's rhetoric. For they are surely attempting to

identify *particular* omissions from the center and making *specific* proposals to change the consensus, which is as it should be. But given such aims, deconstruction's generalized strategy is very dangerous: if as a result of feminist and left-wing efforts, male chauvinist and fascist voices become marginalized, will that very fact make them intellectually respectable again? (1989, 96; emphasis as in the source)

In its theoretical form, deconstruction is decontextualized reasoning, and this can imply an indiscriminate levelling of discourses. Causes of the kind mentioned by Ellis can be served and concerns surrounding them addressed only through a contextualized reasoning. The possibility of discursive/conceptual deconstruction is an anti-foundational theoretical aid, not a substitute for contextual reasoning. Drucilla Cornell responds to charges of the above kind: 'Derrida's text leaves us with the infinite responsibility undecidability imposes on us. Undecidability in no way alleviates responsibility. The opposite is the case. We cannot be excused from our own role in history because we could not know so as to be reassured that we were "right" in advance' (1992, 169).

For literary criticism, deconstruction has been, among other things, a seductive invitation to unleash the protean energies of the text,[9] a banner of revolt against the tyranny of closure. Origins, boundaries, axioms, protocols and hermeneutic economies ceased to count. Its own advertising strategy presented the phenomenon as the *Poltergeist* (etymologically, rattling spirit) of literary criticism, a threateningly powerful force which departments of English had to reckon with. Deconstruction also legitimized an uncanonical idiom in which those who glamorously practised it could write about it. However, as Miller points out, Derrida and Paul de Man do not offer a method but provide us with 'exemplary acts of reading' (1995, 80): 'Deconstruction, like any method of interpretation, can only be exemplified, and the examples will of course all differ' (1991, 231). Let us look at a Derrida example. In 'Ulysses Gramophone', a piece to which Gasché grants the status of a philosophical text ('property of philosophy'), Derrida offers a non-linear reading of James Joyce's *Ulysses*. He shows how the book's elements can coalesce in unconventional, non-linear ways to create meaning: Molly Bloom's life-affirming 'yes' in the interior monologue of the 'Penelope' episode, the coda of the book, is read as a belated response to her husband's telephone call to a businessman, Alexander Keyes, in 'Aeolus'. It may be argued that Derrida is able to link Leopold Bloom's telephone call and Molly's 'yes' because *Ulysses* is a fragmentary text whose elements can coalesce in multiple ways (a cluster of dots which can be joined to form several figures) and that this cannot happen with all texts. The text itself self-reflexively illustrates the possibility of creating meaning through making connections between its apparently unrelated parts. Where there is no logical connection, there could be a symbolic one. Within the linear narrative, when Martha Clifford, Leopold Bloom's epistolary love-interest, makes a typographical error in her anonymous letter to him, he pursues its semantic possibilities to affirm the plenitude of the human world around in contrast to the poverty of the other world. She writes: 'I called you naughty boy because *I do not like that other world* [instead of "word"; emphasis added]. Please tell me what is the real meaning of that word? [*sic*]' (Joyce 1984, 5.244–46). Bloom responds to the error several pages later in the Prospect Cemetery, ironically also conveying Joyce's 'this-worldly' religious attitudes: 'There is another world after death named hell. I do not like that other world she wrote. No more do I. Plenty to see and hear and feel yet. Feel live warm beings near you. Let them sleep in their maggoty beds. They are not going to get me this innings. Warm beds: warm fullblooded life' (6.1001–5).

The self-consciously anticipative hermeneutic of *Ulysses* prevents an apparently invalid textual element from remaining invalid by hooking it elsewhere, thus providing an alternative validating logic. In a linear narrative, the elements follow one after the other (*nacheinander*). The reader needs to keep them mentally one next to the other (*nebeneinander*).[10] The text is self-righting because it is self-writing. Owing to the intra-textual magnetism – the potential of the textual elements to club, to hook themselves elsewhere and self-validate – we can say: 'a text of genius makes no mistakes. Its errors are coalitional and are the portals of meaning' (after Stephen's psycho-biographical statement on Shakespeare: 'A man of genius makes no mistakes. His errors are volitional and are the portals of discovery'; Joyce 1984, 9.228–29).

The most lauded of 'Joyce effects' (the title of Derek Attridge's work on the high-modernist author) consists in the change he ushered in our conception of language – particularly, his role in foregrounding the 'plurisignificatory' character of the word. Perhaps, in a lighter vein, we can say: Had there been no Joyce, there would have been no Derrida – 'a mystical estate, an apostolic succession' (Joyce 1984, 9.837-9)! This may be an exaggeration, but, as Julian Wolfreys observes, 'What James Joyce may be said to represent for Derrida is a certain optimum mobilization of equivocacy and undecidability, which Derrida acknowledges in "Two Words for Joyce"' (Wolfreys 1998, 39). The two words in question are from *Finnegans Wake* (1939) – 'He war' – which Derrida subjects to deconstructive analysis: 'He [Humphrey Chimpden Earwicker] makes war' and 'He was' (based on the German meaning of the verb 'war'). With its use of multiple languages, portmanteau words (in the manner of Lewis Carroll), puns and a thoroughly unconventional syntax, the *Wake* came in handy for Derrida. Joyce used puns and portmanteau words as a means of packing enormous masses of telegraphic allusions into a short space in the *Wake*:

> We grisly old Sykos [psychoanalysts] who have done our unsmiling bit on alices [young girls, also an allusion to Lewis Carroll's Alice books] when they were yung [German word for young, also a reference to Carl Gustav Jung, who treated Lucia, Joyce's daughter] and easily freudened [frightened, and a reference to Sigmund Freud] in the penumbra of the procuring room and what oracular compression we have had to apply to them. (1975, 115)

The pleasure of reading the book lies in the possibility of participating in its meaning-making dynamism. Reading becomes a kind of puzzle-solving.

The examples from Joyce given above illustrate two deconstructive features of texts. The first of these features is, as the *Wake* passages show, an undermining of 'mimetic correspondence' (Wolfreys 1998, 17) by what Derrida would call 'excesses' and 'supplements'. As Christopher Norris puts it, 'To deconstruct a text is to draw out conflicting logics of sense and implication, with the object of showing that the text never exactly means what it says or says what it means' (1988, 7). Second, as is the case with the *Ulysses* examples, they demonstrate how the apparently a-logical intra-textual coalitions produce (or destabilize) meaning, which also points to the etymology of the word 'text'. The English word 'text' is derived from the Latin infinitive *texere*, which means 'to weave'. 'Textus' is the past participle form, meaning 'woven'. Meaning and *différance* are a function of textual weaving and unweaving. As Wolfreys rightly points out, 'meaning is context-dependent and the product of a structure rather than a discrete unit, and rather than there being any full meaning inherent in any one term' (1998, 41–42), and 'rhetoric performs its own structure' (22).

What does deconstruction mean for literary research? If we go by Hillis Miller's clarification 'Deconstruction is not a dismantling of the structure of a text but a demonstration that it has already dismantled itself' (1976, 341), the following may appear to be the case. We know the finding in advance. What is singular about a particular deconstructive enterprise is merely the demonstration. The thrill lies in the process of discovering or revealing the ways in which the text has 'dismantled itself'. If this is the case, as we saw earlier, it is return of 'deductive (syllogistic) reasoning' in another form. This is where the self-deconstructive character of deconstruction becomes significant. Derrida illustrated this by an estrangingly inconsistent emphasis on his own 'masterwords' so that they did not 'congeal' (Spivak 1974, lxxi). They become mere 'figures'. Deconstruction consciously takes a position against programmatic replication and emphasizes irreducible singularity: 'We cannot bring an idea of reading to a text ahead of its being read. The particularity of the text precludes the possibility of a theory or method of reading' (Wolfreys 1998, 50–51). Deconstruction is different every time we invoke it in relation to a text. As Wolfreys urges, 'we have constantly to be on our guard against falling into those programmatic, conventional, institutionally approved modes of thought where everything is decided in advance, everything is planned and given some kind of anticipatory articulation, a strait jacket with which to welcome the guest' (190). The guest could be the text or deconstruction itself.

The redeeming feature of deconstruction is that it is a huge paradox. Fidelity to the rules of the game in practice undermines the theory of the game. Even as we recognize its ontological slipperiness, we cannot let go its terminology. Deconstruction has proven itself a vividly illustrative example of the ability of any idea to turn on itself. Its legacy lies (no pun intended) in this admirable paradox. That is why Geoffrey Bennington maintains that the only way of respecting Derrida's thought is to betray it (1993, 316). The legacy of deconstruction for academia is a culture of perpetual (self-)questioning. It has provided a repertoire to approach the word and the world with scepticism. If, today, we unfortunately find that scepticism is mistaken for critical intelligence, fortunately this unwritten maxim itself is liable to such self-questioning.

3.7 Why Not 'Work' *and* 'Text'?

According to Roland Barthes's critical narrative, the transition from conventional criticism to post-structuralism is a movement from 'work' to 'text' – that is, a shift from looking at a novel or a poem or a play as an entity with fixed meanings, mainly decided by the author for eternity, to a view of the same entity as an endless play of linguistic signifiers, whose meanings are open. The work is about the past, in as much as you want it. The text is about limitless future potential. The work is anchored in literary archaeology. The text is futurological. The work requires excavation; the text elicits speculation. As far as practical criticism is concerned, this distinction between the work and the text is one of the *données* or conceptual frames of reference. We say different sets of things – each set being internally diverse as well – on the same piece depending upon our decision to view it as either work or text. In constructing an argument, it is perfectly possible to blend the work- and text-premises as easily as the undecidability-thesis can combine with the ideology-thesis. In fact, a lot of literary research, knowingly or unknowingly, manifests such combinations.

Though M. H. Abrams claims that 'authors write to be understood', post the theory of intentional fallacy, even the intention to be understood appears irrelevant. It may be remembered that the objections to 'biographical criticism', typical of the work-mode, arose in response to the practice, in a part of academia, of overwhelmingly redundant collection of biographical data. As Stein Haugom Olsen observes, 'It came [...] as reaction against what its opponents variously called "the factualist system", "the biographical fashion in criticism", or the "personal heresy", and was directed against what was seen as an accumulation of facts about authors that had little or no bearing on the understanding or appreciation of the works produced by those authors' (Olsen 2010, 438). Martin Schütze, whom Olsen cites, explains,

> The principal and characteristic manifestation of the factualistic perversion of poetic-artistic meaning is the insistence on exclusively external documentation of literary meaning. Any sort of authenticated record by the author and his contemporaries concerning the occasions, the intentions, the values, of his works, and the actual and supposed experiences, opinions of persons and events, moral and intellectual attitudes; letters written and received by the author, contemporary criticism, attitudes toward him; records of conversations; any documents bearing upon his modes of life and work, are treated as primary evidence of literary meaning. (1968, 238–39)

However, authorial history and even her/his personal mythology are important to interpreting literature if we choose the work-mode.

Autopsy of the dead author (biopsy for those who still believe her/him alive) will yield us significant information concerning artistic evolution, compositional choices and synthesis of the world-forces. It seems a strange paradox and an intellectual lacuna to see that despite the prolific character of writings on literary texts, criticism is yet to come to grips with the delicate, elusive and often inscrutable compositional process. The process by which life becomes art is not an evident one and needs for its exposition textual, historical and philosophical research. Genetic criticism, which endeavours to fill the lacuna, may apparently be considered as basing itself upon the work-premise. But matters are a bit more complex with genetic criticism, and we shall discuss this in detail in the next section of this chapter. Genetic criticism does not content itself with one particular state of the text, as most approaches in literary studies do, but focuses on the process by which the text came to be. The chief concern here is not the 'final' text but the reconstruction and analysis of the writing process. The genetic approach is a form of textual scholarship which focuses on the roles of all concerned with the making, distribution and reception of the text, including publisher, printer, bookseller and critics, in shaping the text. Geneticists are interested in what

Jean Bellemin-Noël calls the *avant-texte*: a critical gathering of the writer's notes, sketches, drafts, manuscripts, typescripts, proofs and correspondence. In practice, genetic criticism is a combination of biographical studies of writers, including the dynamic cognitive processes involved in writing, textual criticism and intertextual studies (what were called 'influences' under the now-obsolete 'source-studies' as well as the 'hypertexts' of the structural studies à la Gérard Genette). It is interested in the chronology of writing and looks at the successive states of a book – alterations, exclusions, interpolations and approximations. It is a unique approach to literature in that 'it aims to restore a temporal dimension to the study of literature' (Deppman, Ferrer and Groden 2004, 2). The emphasis is on 'the chain of events in a writing process' (2). Genetic studies aspire to write the 'biographies' of books. It studies how the literary texts which are celebrated today – and even those which are not so celebrated – actually took their present shape. For example, what was Salman Rushdie reading when he wrote a certain chapter of *Midnight's Children* (1981), and how did it influence the process and product of writing? This work-mode research has tremendous implications for meaning and interpretation. If, for instance, James Joyce uses a book listed in the *Index Librorum Prohibitorum* (an official list of books which Roman Catholics were forbidden to read), does it not have a bearing on the conception of his apostate autobiographical character, Stephen Dedalus? (Hans Walter Gabler, the master geneticist who produced the critical and synoptic editions of Joyce's texts, gave this example in a discussion on genetic criticism). Equally important are the author's comments on his works. If one factors in Joyce's emphasis that the title of his first novel was a portrait of the artist *as a young man*, one may easily see the ironic distance between the author and his alter ego. Historical meanings of words are another useful analytical component in the work-mode. Recall Raymond Williams' observation on the word 'neighbour' in Shakespeare (see 1.3). New Historicist interest in modes of cultural production and circulation also calls for the work-mode.

The comparatively new paradigm of the text irretrievably dismisses an authorial cogito and replaces it with a reader cogito. In the text-mode, the entity which is the object of our study is an amorphous kite in the air, a rudderless object let loose in the fluid medium of language. Since language is 'plurisignificative', since the signifier and the signified have only a gliding relationship, readers have absolute freedom to derive new meanings, even those which the authors are incapable of dreaming. But the reader is not as autonomous as is assumed. Codes of interpretation are culturally acquired, and therefore, envisage relativism only of a collective type. Some critics are apprehensive that the text-mode also implies suspension of logic and plausibility, in the interest of freedom. This freedom varies with the nature of the text. For example, in 'Ulysses Gramophone', Derrida is able to link Leopold Bloom's telephone call in 'Aeolus' and Molly Bloom's 'yes' in 'Penelope' because *Ulysses* is a fragmentary text whose elements can coalesce in non-linear ways; this cannot happen with all texts. But if the umbrella in 'The Oxen of the Sun' episode can mean a contraceptive, of course, Alexander Pope's *The Rape of the Lock* has elements in it to suggest that it could be about chastity-belts (courtesy for the real-life classroom anecdote: Sam Slote, Trinity College Dublin).

Having said that, we may agree intuitively that meanings are to be found somewhere along the continuum of authorial intention and free interpretation. (Personally, I have found 'spectrum' a better schema than 'binaries'.) Is there something called 'plausible meanings'? Of course, a signifier signifies variously. But the significations are not so different as to resemble the imagined communicative gesture of a Tyrannosaurus rex to a jaguar, two species which did not have a chance to live at the same point of time in evolutionary history. It is said that meanings are culturally relative and that this renders cross-cultural understanding impossible. Cross-cultural discourse is *not* an impossibility: 'In your culture x means x_1, with connotative meanings x_2, x_3 and x_4. In my culture, x means y, with connotative meanings y_1, y_2 and y_3. We need to keep this in mind when we read each other's texts'.

3.8 From Textual Being to Avant-Textual Becoming: A Temporal Ontology for Texts

The interregnum between the emergence of a new approach to texts on the critical horizon and its dismissal as just another academic fad has been, more often than not, rather brief. Conversely, academia may also be bowled over by an approach within a short span of time. The reasons for prompt dismissals, as for instant acceptance, could be manifold. The premises of the new approach may be unacceptable in such a field as literary studies where critics belong to just too many persuasions. It need not always be the superficial resistance of those trained in previous critical methods, who consider their approaches sufficient to deal with texts, and, as such, view the new-fangled ones redundant. The dismissals could also arise from the difference in the nature of critical labour required. Philosophically oriented literary scholars may reject – or consider as 'necessary' but 'insufficient' – an approach on account of what they reckon to be its fundamental fallacies, for example, Harold Bloom's objection to what he calls the 'School of Resentment', which we shall discuss in detail in the final chapter.

What is the case with genetic criticism? Samuel Johnson remarked in 1779 that

> it is pleasant to see great works in their seminal state, pregnant with latent possibilities of excellence; nor could there be any more delightful entertainment to trace their gradual growth and expansion, and to observe how they are sometimes suddenly advanced by accidental hints, and sometimes slowly improved by steady meditation. (1977, 407)

In an article entitled 'History or Genesis?' Louis Hay observes: 'Manuscripts have something new to tell us: it is high time we learned to make them speak' (1996, 207). What is new about the manuscripts that genetic criticism can reveal? Can they offer anything more than textual scholarship does, or something more than 'delightful entertainment'? For too long in academic literary history it was taken for granted that the book in hand is the sole artefact one needed to be concerned with in interpreting it, critiquing it and relating it to larger extra-textual concerns. A staticity was assumed at least till one picked it up for reading, the dynamism taking over, even in post-structuralist readings, only after this. Of course, there have been exceptions to this. Many celebrated written texts went through various oral versions before being compiled and edited for the modern reader. Homer's epics are cited as typical examples of this protogenetic process. So are many sacred texts. For instance, as the Documentary Hypothesis – also known as the Wellhausen Hypothesis – has it, the Torah was derived from several independent and parallel narratives which were subsequently combined into the current form by a series of redactors (editors). This hypothesis, an exercise in what is called historical criticism of scriptures, has identified four sources of the text, which, chronologically listed, are: the Yahwist source (J), the Elohist source (E), the Deuteronomist (D) and the Priestly source (P). The earlier text was thoroughly edited by what is called the P source in Babylonian captivity, which gave Judaism its uncompromising monotheistic character – an attempt to explain suffering of the chosen people in terms of the abandoning of monotheistic faith in Yahweh. Studies on scriptural genesis, revisions and interpolations have had a bearing on the understanding of religion itself. As I argue in chapter 6 of *The Ontology of Gods: An Account of Enchantment, Disenchantment, and Re-Enchantment*, this significantly foregrounds the temporal development of religious systems. Ordinarily, these systems are considered atemporal:

> [Religious] faith depends to a considerable extent upon the capability of the religious system to make a coherent synchronic presentation to the subject of its own complex diachronic development. The efficacy of the

system emerges from the erased consciousness of its ideational origin and complex temporal evolution. The system hypostatises a process into an image. (George 2017a, 56)

As a result, at any given point of time, the religious subject takes the world-picture that is given in the sacred text to be ontologically preset. But the genesis and development of textual elements tell a different story. For instance, the flood and creation stories of the Torah, which were probably absent in the original Mosaic text, were borrowed from Mesopotamian myths (Armstrong 1999, 14, 19). The Tower of Babel is a version of the Ziggurat, the Sumerian temple tower with stone ladders for devotees to climb up and 'meet' their gods, such as Marduk (15, 465). In the course of this temporal evolution Yahweh, probably a Midianite deity, whom Moses encountered in the desert, blends with Elohim (which itself is a plural noun), the creator of the world, to appear as one God (29). The Hebrew Book of Job parallels a Babylonian Job. Similarly, historical Christianity sublated the content and spirit of antecedent religions, and made hybrid use of ideational resources from almost everywhere (George 2017a, 57). Built upon the system of the monotheistic Judaic deity and the Hebraic and other forms of messianic anticipation, it created a Triune God out of the Greek Absolute, Semitic conceptions of kingship (the Christ) and Hebrew *ruach* (Spirit).

In literary studies, the genetic approach, in its prototypical form, was initiated by authors themselves. They have tried to critically recapitulate the process of writing, revealing the 'backstage' of the creative performance. We find the origins of genetic criticism in the attempts of Johann Wolfgang von Goethe, Friedrich Schlegel, the English Romantics, William Wordsworth and Samuel Coleridge in particular, and Edgar Allan Poe to recount the processes of artistic growth and literary composition. Coleridge's *Biographia Literaria* and Poe's 'The Philosophy of Composition' (1846; translated into French a decade later by Charles Baudelaire as 'Genèse d'un poème') are among the earliest versions of authorial attempts at delineating the creative-compositional dynamics. Poe's essay 'The Philosophy of Composition', in which he describes the method he employed in writing the poem 'The Raven' and demystifies the creative process, calculating and maximizing every effect, is considered 'one of the foundational texts of French genetic criticism' (Deppman, Ferrer and Groden 2004, 3). These de facto versions notwithstanding, in its present form as a literary critical movement, genetic criticism is an outgrowth of the French structuralist movement and drew upon the new notions of text and textuality inaugurated by post-structuralist thinking. Institut des Textes et Manuscrits Modernes (ITEM), Centre National de la Recherche Scientifique (CNRS), Paris has played a key role in its development. The trends in *critique génétique* are represented by the classic collection of essays entitled *Genetic Criticism: Texts and Avant-Textes* (2004), edited by Jed Deppman, Daniel Ferrer and Michael Groden. Geneticists have studied modernist writers (Yeats, Eliot and Joyce), French writers of several periods (Flaubert, Stendhal, Zola, Proust, Anatole France and Sartre), Victorian novelists such as Emily Brontë and American poets such as Emily Dickinson. Representative titles include Mary Visick's *The Genesis of 'Wuthering Heights'* (1958), John Paterson's *The Making of 'The Return of the Native'* (1960), A. Walton Litz's *The Art of James Joyce: Method and Design in 'Ulysses' and 'Finnegans Wake'* (1961), David Hayman's *A First-Draft Version of 'Finnegans Wake'* (1963), Jon Stallworthy's *Between the Lines: Yeats's Poetry in the Making* (1963), Curtis Bradford's *Yeats at Work* (1965), Michael Groden's *'Ulysses' in Progress* (1977), Helen Gardner's *The Composition of 'Four Quartets'* (1978) and Ralph W. Franklin's *The Manuscript Books of Emily Dickinson* (1981). *Yale French Studies* devoted an issue, entitled *Drafts*, to genetic criticism.

What is singular and complex (that is, in contradistinction to other schools of criticism) about genetic criticism is that it not only extends the hermeneutic scope of a text but also enlarges its very definition, sometimes rendering unstable the object of study itself. There is a process behind the book in hand. The text has had many previous states, and every textual element has a prehistory. This raises an ontological question of tremendous significance: What is it that we need to call the text? Can our interpretation of the text confine itself to the final version, or should its basis be expanded to include previous textual versions as well – towards an 'open-ended aesthetic' (Deppman, Ferrer and Groden 2004, 6)? Can there be a genetic hermeneutic? Is the ontology of the text temporally static or dynamic (here we are not discussing the hermeneutic dynamic that is inaugurated exclusively with reading)? Should we bother about a work that might have been? In other words, it is the question of whether the notion of the text should include the *avant-texte* as well. Does it have implications for literary history? If avant-textes are taken into consideration alongside the finished texts, will it lead to a revision of the canon? Can the process, rather than the product, become an alternative criterion for evaluation of literary merit? This may sound a futuristic, if not hypothetical, question, but genetic criticism wittingly or unwittingly places these questions at the centre of literary criticism. Alternatively, is the reconstruction of the writing process an endeavour and reward in itself, without a substantial bearing on hermeneutic questions? No doubt the last can be a self-sufficiently legitimate critical enterprise. Most of the apprehensions about this school are a 'so-what?' response. Hence we shall focus here on the interpretive implications of the avant-textual enterprise. This is not an exposition of genetic criticism; the focus here is its bearing on what we already do and can do. What does getting inside the genes of texts imply? We shall first look at a few cases and then raise some pertinent questions on the implications of geneticism for a philosophical understanding of literary texts and their interpretation.

Let us consider a few examples of avant-textual studies which come up with interpretive insights from the collection of essays edited by Deppman, Ferrer and Groden. Raymonde Debray Genette, a Flaubert scholar and a proponent of narratological genetics, in her article 'Flaubert's "A Simple Heart", or How to make an Ending: A Study of the Manuscripts' (Deppman, Ferrer and Groden 2004, 69–95), having sifted through the avant-textual data of the story 'Un Coeur simple', puts forward a thesis on the author's negotiations with literary and cultural models with regard to the death of the main character (Félicité) – that Flaubert made a gradual, ambivalent ending of his story 'by [intertextually] ignoring or integrating key elements from pagan, Christian, baroque, beatific, Romantic, mystic, scientific, saintly, and other stories and pictures of death' (69). Flaubert's 'anti-romanticism and impersonality' were the culminating rather than starting point of the process indicated by such a 'long, laborious construction' (70). Genette illustrates the influence of the genetic dimension upon meaning with examples of 'two different isotopic lines that will enter into conflict and provoke a constant disruption of meaning that only the last folio will resolve' (74). Rather than the ending completing the beginning of the story in a traditional manner, 'the incipit multiplies the signs of closure while the excipit multiplies the signs of opening' (72). Genette's genetic work problematizes a simple reading of the story founded on Félicité's saintliness and formulaic beatific death into a complex one which sees ironization of a Christian cliché in a change from orthodox to heterodox representation, a fusion of the profane and the sacred, and a mésalliance of saintliness, sensuality and mental confusion. The text of 'Un Coeur simple' itself is revealed as 'a double tissue with a novel of manners on the front and a hagiographic story on the back' (87).

Similarly, in an article entitled 'Proust's "Confessions of a Young Girl": Truth or Fiction?' (Deppman, Ferrer and Groden 2004, 171–92), Catherine Viollet, primarily a linguist, argues that

> Proust was wrestling personally with how to express or confess his own sexuality and that this private struggle was complexly and perhaps unwittingly inscribed in the genesis of his fiction […] Through meticulous genetic work, she [Viollet] reconstructs the ways Proust wrote himself so deeply into his female character that he ultimately described 'her' sexuality in unmistakably masculine terms. She reveals, too, that when Proust vacillated over the age and sex of his transgressive fictional character, he may have well been struggling to understand and control

the way such indices affect the social judgment of character in both his fiction and his life. (2004, 171)

Demonstrating how astute linguistic observations could produce genetic patterns, Viollet does a comparative analysis of the manuscripts of Proust's short stories 'Avant la nuit' and 'La Confession d'une jeune fille' and identifies the 'way Proust (unthinkingly?) misspelled past participles – parts of speech that in French reveal one's gender as *either* masculine or feminine [these errors are scattered throughout the drafts]' (2004, 172; italics as in the source). Her linguistic attention to 'the gender of pronouns, the use of the first-person narrative, and the fluctuating subtleties of Proust's use of general and intimate forms of "we"' enables her to 'demonstrate [...] several strategies for interpreting different layers of text that are somehow "explicitly" fictional and "virtually" autobiographical' (172). One of her findings is that 'while the heroine's sex is clearly defined from the start, her grammatical gender varies' (181). Extrapolating from such microelements, Viollet points out that

> the indefinite article 'of *an*other' sex is not as trivial as it seems and cannot equate to 'of the other sex'. Whether or not it alludes to the 'third sex', in vogue at that time, the use of this definite article in fact represents a double transgression. 'Of another sex' contravenes the linguistic norm and subverts this norm: to escape biological bipartition amounts to questioning explicitly the bi-categorizing system of thought. 'Of another sex' also has the effect of generalizing the range of the assertion by relativizing the sex of the subject himself. (178)

Indeed an avant-textual analysis provides additional grounds on which to extrapolate. But, more importantly, here is a spark in the part that eventually illuminates the whole, that too coming from outside of what has been traditionally considered the boundary of the text, which also sets at play a dialectic between the micro- and macro-dimensions of the text's signifying cycle, rendering the traditional 'hermeneutic circle' even more complex. The same could be said of Amuth Grésillon's study of Proust's complex use of grammatical temporal markers 'still' and 'already' in *À la recherche du temps perdu* (another article included in the volume edited by Deppman et al.), translated into English both as *Remembrance of Things Past* and *In Search of Lost Time*.

James Joyce's *Ulysses*, whose composition is a history in itself, was an inevitable stimulant for the critical paradigm shift from textual 'being' to avant-textual 'becoming'. *James Joyce and the Making of Ulysses* (1934), a memoir written by Frank Budgen, English painter and Joyce's friend, is probably the first 'genetic' record of the compositional process of the magnum opus. Budgen tells us about the author's search for the most appropriate syntax, 'an order [of words] in every way appropriate', which would add the seduction motive from the 'Lestrygonians' episode of Homer's *Odyssey* to the scene where Bloom goes to lunch. The resultant sentences are: 'Perfume of embraces all him assailed. With hungered flesh obscurely, he mutely craved to adore' (Budgen 1960, 20; Joyce 1984, 8.638–39). An understanding of the compositional process behind *Ulysses* can make explicit the capacity of textual elements to coalesce and cross-validate (which we already discussed), for example, the significance of the apparently erroneous use of the word 'crosstree' in the 'Proteus' episode (3.504):

> 'You know, Joyce' [Budgen] said, 'When Stephen sees that three-mastered schooner's sails brailed up to her crosstrees'.
>
> 'Yes', he said. 'What about it?'
>
> 'Only this. I sailed on schooners of that sort once and the only word we ever used for the spars to which the sails are bent was "yards". "Crosstrees" were the lighter spars fixed near the lower masthead. Their function was to give purchase to the topmast standing rigging'.
>
> 'Thank you for pointing it out', [Joyce] said. 'There's no sort of criticism I more value than that. But the word "crosstrees" is essential. It comes in later on and I can't change it. After all, a yard is also a crosstree for the onlooking landlubber'. (Budgen 57)

And crosstree does recur in the pattern of the 'Scylla and Charybdis' episode, where Stephen propounds his Shakespeare theory: 'Who put upon by His fiends, stripped and whipped, was nailed like bat to barndoor, starved on crosstree' (Joyce 1984, 9.494–6). The passage is a parody of the Apostle Creed, and the erroneous usage is essential to the Christ symbolism of the book, and to the theme of the Passion of the artist (both Shakespeare and Joyce). It may be argued that the above-mentioned kind of findings is possible without a genetic study. One response to this argument is that most Joyce criticism has a genetic subtext. But a better one, though this may revive critical memories of the authorial cogito/intention (perhaps we will never be able to geneticize and contextualize without considering the author), is that an understanding of Joyce's *design* for the book – what exactly is being written? – has a bearing on its interpretation. Why would a meticulous writer, who made explicit his self-imposed meticulousness with regard to his narrative intentions and aesthetic practice in conversations, letters and the like, let the textual errors remain where they are?[11] Some genetic work on *Ulysses* relates textual elements to its author's personal circumstances. For instance, Roy Gottfried's *Joyce's Iritis and the Irritated Text: The Dis-Lexic Ulysses* (1995) reads the errors in *Ulysses* in conjunction with Joyce's poor eyesight. But I attribute them to a conscious decision, to a confidence that the erroneous elements will fit into the text's ever-expanding network of meaning. *Ulysses* is an elaborate contrivance, an overstretched network of correspondences, motifs and symbols – a network capable of expansion and exacerbation beyond any assumed authorial intention. Joyce had several schemata for the book, which he shared with friends and friendly scholars such as Herbert Gorman, Valery Larbaud, Carlo Linati, Stuart Gilbert and Edmund Wilson. The one given by Gilbert in his 1931 book *James Joyce's Ulysses: A Study* sets for each episode an hour of the day, a scene, a science or art, a dominant colour, a symbol, an allegorical sense, a narrative technique and Homeric correspondences (Gilbert 1955, 30). Many textual elements which are inappropriate and deviant when the book is seen as a linear mimetic narrative attain validity when they are seen as part of a network of meaning. A textual element which is a mistake of one kind or the other when seen in isolation proves not only appropriate but also essential in combination with other textual elements.

Further, as we saw earlier, the self-consciously anticipative hermeneutic of *Ulysses* prevents an apparently invalid element from remaining invalid by hooking it elsewhere, thus providing an alternative validating logic. In a linear narrative, the elements follow one after the other (*nacheinander*). The reader needs to keep them mentally one next to the other (*nebeneinander*). Jean-Michel Rabaté, a Joyce critic, has made a case for the 'ideal genetic reader' in the context of expanding archives[12] – 'an extraordinarily creative reader who approaches the esoteric text [*Finnegans Wake*] through the mass of notebooks and typescripts and can transform the text in terms of its pre-texts' (Bulson 2006, 122). In the case of his later work *Finnegans Wake* (1939), perhaps one of the most esoteric works written in literary history, a lot of criticism was generated and invited during the gestation period, then called 'Work in Progress'. Samuel Beckett's *Our Exagmination Round His Factification for Incamination of Work in Progress*, a 1929 collection of critical essays and two letters, is a prominent example of this category of criticism.

In *Ulysses in Progress*, Michael Groden shows how the high-modernist magnum opus was not the result of implementing a pre-written schema but Joyce made it up as he went along, as evident in the presence of three different 'styles' in the book. Does this make a difference? In fact, it does tell us something vital about the elusively dynamic compositional process. As Pierre-Marc de Biasi observes, 'An author may not even decide upon the focus of the definitive text until very late in the writing process, after working for a long time on passages that have no place in the final project' (Deppman, Ferrer and Groden 2004, 49). Writers often conceive a provisional goal, tentative plans, and make initial choices, but the contingent, constrained, often capricious and multifarious ways in which they pursue these – trudging along with disappointments, reactions, accidents, alternatives and alterations, and all the elements of natural selections in the genetic evolution – redefine the goal, and the effects are evident in the final product. A retrospective glance in turn can throw interesting insights on the negotiations between life and art. The writing process, and all artistic creation, is subject to what I call a *telos paradox*. Perhaps this is true of the trajectory of human life itself. With obvious courtesy to Jean-Paul Sartre, just as through actual 'existence', making choices and exercising freedom, one defines one's essence, myriad actual decisions – negations, negotiations, alterations, additions and substitutions – in the process of writing, the work attains its *quidditas*. It attains an unpregiven shape through writing itself. The point is that writing, in all its dimensions – linguistic, rhetorical, tropological, cognitive, cultural, idiosyncratic and so on – has its own dynamic which can draw into its vortex the myriad potential elements and configures them in a way that is beyond any pre-fixed plan. How much of a freedom does the writer have in the process? Indeed writing is an overdetermined process. But it is not deterministic. The writer works with an inherited linguistic repertoire, set of cultural codes and models, literary conventions and received ideological notions. What makes the creative process dynamic is their singular configuration – in memory, in imagination, in calculation, in craft.

Does genetic criticism belong to the work-mode or the text-mode? As stated at the beginning of this section, it was writers themselves who wanted the world to know about the intricacies of their own creative act. What if there is a conflict between what the author and the text say? This has practical implications for literary research. A few years ago, a PhD scholar working on *Chronicles of Narnia* (1950-56) wanted to argue that the work of C. S. Lewis, widely understood as a Christian apologist, actually evinced a self-conscious amalgamation and recirculation of literary tropes which also mediated matters of faith. She was told by a Lewis critic that the author himself would not have approved of what she claimed. She undertook a study of Lewis's notes, drafts, readings and correspondence, and apparently proved her point. Who knows Dante could well be an agnostic literary craftsman merely modifying the Greek trope of *katabasis* (the hero's descent into the underworld) for late-medieval Christian consumption. In such cases, the avant-textes pave the way for a grounded interpretation of the author and his work – in the work-mode.

With its strong empirical interest in the 'materiality of texts' (Deppman, Ferrer and Groden 2004, 1), and the requirements of rigorous archival work, genetic approach is 'tangible': 'Like old-fashioned philology or textual criticism, it examines tangible documents such as writers' notes, drafts and proof corrections, but its real object is something much more abstract – not the existing documents but the movement of writing that must be inferred from them' (2). It deals with the creative process at its tangible best though the process that it deals with has been traditionally considered most intangible. Perhaps it may be considered the tangible dimension of an otherwise intangible process. The empirical study of manuscripts has earned genetic criticism the reputation of a 'hard science', perhaps in a fulfilment of the scientific aspirations of the humanities, and accords its findings a degree of positivist verifiability, which may assign it to the work-mode of literary criticism. But geneticism is double edged and can operate both ways. It is beyond 'hard science', whose requirements it is believed to fulfil, and requires intuitive intelligence and creative speculation, as with other modes of literary criticism, both in the reconstruction of the writing process, in deducing the underlying cognitive processes (if this at all is an objective), and working out the hermeneutic implications of amorphous masses of documents. Deppman, Ferrer and Groden, in the introduction to their book, make this double-edgedness explicit in a series of antithetic parallelisms, the most significant of which in this context is: 'It grows out of structuralist and post-structuralist notion of "text" as an infinite play of signs, but it accepts a teleological model of textuality and constantly confronts the question of authorship' (2). Though its empiricism might apparently argue against the free play of signifiers, it is compatible with deconstruction. With its expansion of textual criticism to pre-texts, often without the usual hierarchical preferences between them, it contests the meanings which were otherwise believed to be generated, say as the structuralists and New Critics claimed, in a more or less settled fashion within the self-enclosed system of the text. This is also the premise of deconstruction. While deconstruction locates the source of destabilization in the nature of language, genetic criticism bases it on broadening the textual field. The pan-textual field, consisting now of both texts and avant-textes, vastly expands the plane on which the gliding interactions between the signifier and the signified can occur and thereby destabilize meaning. In an 'avant-textual deconstruction', we look for a '*diachronous* play of signifiers' (Deppman, Ferrer and Groden 2004, 5; italics as in the source) than a synchronous one. The final text becomes just yet another entity on the field of temporal unfolding.

How does genetic criticism stand vis-à-vis the deductive reasoning that has crept into literary studies with the overdependence on theory? Of course, as stated earlier, it adds a temporal dimension to both our assumptions about the text and the responses it elicits. But genetic criticism stands in contrast to the above scenario in many ways. (I hold no brief for any particular school.) First it offers only minimal theory, in the sense that it does not have a readymade finding, which can be replicated, to offer as the final product of research. Put otherwise, it has only a minimal premise which opens up the way for actual research on texts and avant-textes. Except perhaps for the specific methodology and the academic disciplines invoked, each genetic enterprise is unique. It is not reductivistic and avoids the fallacy of cognitive ease associated with the application-type research to a great extent and of theorizing from thin air. On the contrary, it is paradigmatic of the actual, detailed labours which are required to come up with any thesis on the texts.

Genetic criticism is not an alternative to any other criticism. In a way, the genetic enterprise is both a meta-critical exercise that problematizes the notions of the text and a para-critical one, which can take advantage of, and feed into, any particular kind of criticism. As Deppman, Ferrer and Groden clarify, 'It cooperates closely with many different forms of literary study – narratology, linguistic analysis, psychoanalytic approaches of various kinds, sociocriticism, deconstruction, gender theory, and so on' (2004, 2). Tracking consistencies and changes through the several versions of the text in question can aid the claims of any school. A psychoanalytic geneticist can work on the patterns of desire and fantasy, of displacement and repression that run through the drafts, manuscripts and typescripts. A Marxist geneticist can examine in the avant-textual material how a writer negotiates the ideological tensions and contradictions of her/his society in consonance with writerly compulsions. A feminist geneticist may trace negotiations and negations of patriarchy and socially constructed gender roles through such material. Genetic criticism is primarily aesthetic (in a larger sense) but can take on political dimensions.

If we are able to envision a genetic approach to texts in a larger sense, that is, as something more than compiling the avant-textes, placing it in historical circumstances, social milieu and cultural contexts, study institutional influences and include relation between individuals and collectivities, we may find answers to more elusive, intriguing questions concerning the fundamentals of writing – the word-world relation. A work of this kind in the volume edited by Deppman, Ferrer and Groden is Henri Mitterand's 'Genetic Criticism and Cultural History: Zola's *Rougon-Macquart* Dossiers'. For example, what is the relationship between the character of the ghost in Hamlet and the change in world view ushered in by the Protestant Reformation? What does creativity under duress mean? What different critical parameters do prison diaries or Dalit writing in India demand?[13] Sometime ago, a prospective researcher approached the Department of English Literature at my university with a doctoral proposal on the suicide notes written by farmers in the Indian state of Maharashtra for whom life had become impossible due to drought and debts. She was not admitted to the doctoral programme. Take a better-known example: Anne Frank's *The Diary of a Young Girl*, which was mostly written in the Secret Annex. Philippe Lejeune elucidates the strictly empirical part of such writing. According to Lejeune, 'A diary, if it is a real diary, has no avant-texte'

(Deppman, Ferrer and Groden 2004, 205). But there are other considerations here. A diary is popularly given as an example of a text which was not originally written with the intention of being read (as literature). But Anne did think of publishing her private thoughts after she heard the announcement of Gerrit Bolkestein, the Minister for Arts, Science and Education, on behalf of the Dutch government-in-exile that he intended to create a public record of Dutch citizens' oppression under Nazi occupation. What difference does the anticipation of readership make to the writing process? Studies of the production of a text and of its reception are complementary and continuous, and small wonder reception aesthetic is part of the genetic approach. As Lejeune points out, 'As soon as the possibility of publication arises, the text of a diary becomes an avant-texte, a rough draft that needs polishing up or a sick person who needs help getting dressed' (208). And interventions, both by the writer and others, do make changes to the text in the process of publication:

> Anne Frank was herself the first person to write her own *Diaries*. During the last three months of her stay at the Annex, she almost entirely rewrote the diary of the preceding two years, with the intention of publishing it herself as soon as the war was over. Thus *two* texts of the *Diary* exist, both in Anne's hand [...] Some of the original diary's notebooks have been lost, and Anne had not finished the rewriting when she was arrested. In order to construct a coherent book, in accordance with Anne's plans, her father had to perform a kind of structural rewrite. The Dutch critical edition gives us all we need to follow the two rewrites: Anne's, then her father's. (212; italics as in the source)

Otto Frank, Anne's father, did remove the passages that dealt with the sexual aspects of his daughter's adolescent development and also her uneasy relationship with her mother, Edith Frank. There is, however, much more to writing than these matter-of-fact descriptions convey, which needs further investigation with the tools of many more disciplines than genetic criticism already uses.

Let us conclude this section with an example to illustrate how an understanding of the deeper sources of writing can illuminate the rift between the rhetorical efficacy of formulaic critical propensities that prepare procrustean critical beds for texts to rest, on the one hand, and what 'the case' is, on the other. Drawing upon Hayden White's postmodern philosophy of history, Richard Poirier (1968) explains self-parody in Joyce and Nabokov saying that it stems from the awareness that literature is no longer the primary source of fictions. History itself is a fictional construct, and all narratives, historical and fictional, are tentative constructs. Literary self-parody results from this loss of primacy. But those who know the *Lebenswelt* out of which Joyce's texts emerged – he punned on his own name to be 'shame's voice' and 'germ's choice' – recognize their self-parody to be a complex imaginative output of several ingredients: his degenerate home, his difficult relationship with Ireland and Catholicism, his position as a colonial subject, the strategies of the subaltern, his messianic fantasies, the comic literary pedigree of the Western literary world, particularly Rabelais, the Irish bull and his own joco-serious *Weltanschauung*.

3.9 The Calculi of Reasoning in Literary Studies

So, what do we do with texts? There are more things about the word and the world than are articulated in our literary theory. There is something very fluid in the world process and human perception which renders many new endeavours possible. To learn what we can say about literature, we need to know the calculi of literary reasoning. Most forms of literary reasoning are 'analogous reasoning', not a cause-and-effect one. If the mode of reasoning is analogous, we can build an argument connecting stanzaic structure with social structure. Let me give a few examples for analogous reasoning. Fredric Jameson argues in his book *Marxism and Form* (1971) that Joyce's *Ulysses* is structured in a way that replicates the totalizing logic of capitalism. Indeed, as we saw earlier, the high-modernist magnum opus is an elaborately schematized work. Nothing is left out of the schema. Jameson's argument is a case of analogous reasoning. No cause-effect chain of reasoning can establish a connection between social and literary patterns. The same holds true for the connection which Enda Duffy theorizes between the textual concealing of quotations in *Ulysses*, one inside another, and the clandestine nature of intelligence gathering in colonial Dublin (1994, 23–26). Similarly, looking at the modernist linguistic estrangement of reality in *Ulysses*, we are free to claim that artistic transmutation functions as an anticipative analogue for social transformation. Realism, through its naturalization of the status quo, makes it appear unalterable. Non-realistic representation draws attention to the constructed character of social reality. It indicates that social reality is also a human creation, like fictional reality, and hence can be otherwise. Joyce's foregrounding of the constructed character of his fictional discourse is also meant to show that it is through human agency and intervention that lived reality is made and, therefore, can be unmade and re-made. The objective of Joycean estrangement, as that of Brechtian estrangement (*Verfremdung*), is to provide the much-needed critical sense wherein lies the trigger to 'mankind's infinite capacity for improvement' (Brecht 1964, 13).

In the analogous mode of reasoning, it is also possible to draw second-order inferences. For instance, in *Ulysses*, on several occasions Leopold Bloom feels his body – the cheek, the hair, the forehead, the belly and the pelvic region – with his hands and smells its odours. It is perfectly possible to infer that it is the loss of this immediacy with one's own embodied self that makes people lose any possible affinity with others, inflict torture and pain on them and renders gas chambers and torture cells possible. The domain of literary reasoning is a discursive space for various levels of extrapolation and bold speculation. The domain affords several freedoms. No hard-and-fast rule obtains regarding the choice of inquiries and approaches. What we might call pettifogging in common parlance might be a legitimate and respectable critical practice. 'How many times does the soap appear in *Ulysses*?' is an academic question! Doctoral dissertations can be written on the scatology of texts. The criteria by which one determines the validity of a critical statement are also open to historical evolution.

Notes

1. Theoretically, it is possible sequentially though not simultaneously.
2. Kant's twelve categories are divided into four sets of three: (1) of quantity: unity, plurality and totality; (2) of quality: reality, negation and limitation; (3) of relation: substance-and-accident, cause-and-effect and reciprocity; (4) of modality: possibility, existence and necessity (qtd. in Russell 1967, 708).
3. The Gestalt principles of perception include the figure-ground relationship (humans focus either on the figure or on the background against which the figure rests), the law of *prägnanz* (humans tend to interpret ambiguous or complex images as simple and complete), uniform connectedness (elements with uniform visual features are perceived as related than those with disparate characteristics), closure (humans tend to look for a single, recognizable pattern), proximity (elements placed close to one another are perceived to be more related than those placed apart) and similarity (similar things are perceived to be more related than dissimilar things).
4. Peter Mackey's innovative work examines the trivial and the random elements of Joyce's *Ulysses* in terms of chaos theory, a field of contemporary mathematics. Mackey's analysis bases itself on the premise that slight changes or tiny perturbations in a complex system can produce exponential impact through an extended trajectory. The most famous metaphor for the phenomenon is found in the title of Edward Lorenz's 1979 address to the annual meeting of the American Association for the Advancement of Science, 'Predictability: Does the Flap of a Butterfly's Wings in Brazil Set Off a Tornado in Texas?'
5. In fact, there are historical contexts where essences (the sacredness of all human life, here) have helped, as in the case of Martin Luther King, Jr's 'spiritual humanism', which formed the ideational basis of the civil rights movement.
6. Tony Davies traces this tradition of internal critique and dialectical contention back to the Renaissance humanists themselves, whose hospitable argumentation and often 'acrimonious fallings out' testify more to heterogeneous, eclectic, open-ended, and

ironic intellectual cultures than 'allegiance to a shared ideological or intellectual programme' (1997, 70) or common values – *coincidentia oppositorum* or harmonious opposition, as Renaissance men called it.

7   A notable work on Derrida and Nietzsche is Paul de Man's 'Nietzsche's Theory of Rhetoric', *Symposium* 28 (1974), pp. 33–51. Of course, Nietzsche wrote about the metaphorical nature of all language and its inability to convey 'truth'. But to John M. Ellis,

> to single out Nietzsche in this way is justified only by the implicit claim that Nietzsche was either the first to express such a view (he was not) or that he was the most influential expounder of such a view before Derrida (also not so) or that his was the most sophisticated, complex, and logically well developed and worked out position of this kind before Derrida (again, obviously not true – Nietzsche's remarks on the subject were brief and undeveloped). (1989, 38n)

Ellis has serious objections to deconstruction and ways in which it is debated. According to him, its tendency to 'avoid the possibility of a [self-] characterization' (1989, 5), which I pointed out at the beginning of this section, is an obstacle in 'refining and sharpening' the debate: 'The claim that deconstruction is a special case, not to be judged or discussed by rational argument and ordinary logic, is a claim that is neither explicated nor really consistently believed and acted upon by those who make it' (14). To Ellis, Derrida's claim that Western intellectual tradition has privileged speech over writing, particularly with its long history of scribes, manuscripts and manuscript studies, is historically inaccurate. The neologisms of deconstruction actually showcase ideas which had long been in circulation. Many deconstructive ideas base themselves on 'a wholesale garbling of Saussurean terminology' (63). Ellis also counters the idea that a signified can also be a signifier as well as the spatio-temporal bases of *différance*, the endless postponement of meaning: 'All words are, in a sense, present for possible choice, and then all but one rendered absent by actual choice; that is how language works' (56). Further, Ellis maintains, while deconstruction's penchant for challenging authoritative interpretation satisfies an 'emotional demand', the fact is that 'a singular authoritative interpretation', the shibboleth of attack, as such never existed for any text.

8   See Gasché (1994, pp. 22–57).
9   The title of this section is borrowed from the 'Proteus' episode of James Joyce's *Ulysses*, where Stephen Dedalus probes 'the ineluctable modality' of thought and experience through the visible and the audible. The Homeric title of the episode comes from the name of the slippery god of water bodies in Greek mythology, whose adjectival form has been repeatedly used as a metaphor for the slipperiness of both language and deconstruction – their refusal to be pinned down.
10 *Nacheinander* and *nebeneinander* are terms that feature in Stephen's interior monologue in the 'Proteus' episode and are a reference to the German aesthetician Gottfried Ephraim Lessing's work *Laocoön* (1766).
11 See Jibu Mathew George, '"Err"meneutic of the "Word" and the "World": Categorizing/Interpreting Errors in James Joyce's *Ulysses*'.
12 See Rabaté, *James Joyce and the Politics of Egoism*, pp. 183, 196. Rabaté made the case in earlier versions of the chapters of his book: 'Back to Beria! Genetic Joyce and Eco's "Ideal Readers"' and 'Pound, Joyce and Eco: Modernism and the Ideal Genetic Reader'.
13 Refer to my discussion of the relation between extreme experience and creativity in Chapter 1.

Chapter 4

THE AESTHETIC AND THE POLITICAL

4.1 The Scandal Called the Aesthetic

It appears too late in the day to ask the question 'What is "good" literature?' It might seem even too late to argue for or against an essentialist definition of literature or literary value. Contemporary literary criticism is weighed in favour of the idea that it is contexts, institutions and discourses which decide the literariness of any piece of speech or writing. We have successfully extended the use of the term 'literature' on the basis of media, genre and sociological criteria to include oral literature, pulp fiction and the writings/cultural practices of many formerly marginalized groups, respectively. It is a critical commonplace that an unconscious system of values lies behind our evaluations of literature, and that this varies from culture to culture and from person to person. For a Marxist critic, this system of values is related to class structure and the intellectual hegemony of the dominant class. For a postcolonial critic, the texts which were considered prestigious and were prescribed for academic study were so, because they were ideological tools of, and in turn received impetus from, the politico-cultural project of imperialism. Similarly, feminists challenge a male-centred canon. Indeed such endeavours have helped to set right the lopsidedness of literary history as well as contemporary priorities.

Apropos the subjective side, indeed the apprehension of literary value is partly a matter of the subject-object symmetry. If this is the case, value – I refuse to categorize it as exclusively 'aesthetic' because there are more aspects to value than pure aesthetic – is located neither exclusively in the reader nor in the text but at the precise point of encounter between them. But the subject is not an autonomous Cartesian one but is constituted in the collective, historically specific discourses. As such, the system of values consists of culturally acquired elements and maybe entangled in the networks of power and ideology. Further, literary values are pluralistic; there are many kinds of excellence.

Is there something called aesthetic quality? Can it be decided at all? If the answer is in the affirmative, how does one decide the quality of a literary work? Can the political be demarcated from the aesthetic? Is there a kind of aesthetic reasoning? If yes, what are its critical premises and procedures? The phenomenon of aesthetic apprehension is mired in a variety of phenomena which belong to both the subject and the object – the reader and the text. This includes the content and organization of the work, leisure, politics, taste and so on. As we saw earlier, it is a matter of experiential symmetry. The symmetry consists of subjective as well as culturally acquired elements. To say that aesthetic apprehension can be entirely taught is to imply that it is only a higher form of 'response conditioning'. In order to make any progress in this field of inquiry, we may have to make at least a temporary move from the plane of discourse and cultural perception to the actual experience of art. Let me re-invoke a concept which we discussed as part of response to literature: delicate epistemes. Art belongs to the realm of delicate epistemes. So does taste, and what is now pejoratively called 'aesthetic sensibility'. Greek *aisthetikos* means 'sensitive' or 'sentient', qualities which we can consider as essential to the apprehension of delicate realities. Apprehension of art is a delicate process, and it is probably due to this fact that Harold Bloom says, 'Pragmatically, aesthetic value can be recognized or experienced, but it cannot be conveyed to those who are incapable of grasping its sensations and perceptions. To quarrel on its behalf is always a blunder' (1995, 17). M. H. Abrams concurs when he observes 'that the ultimate standards of valid critical judgments are not sharp-focus but soft-focus standards which we signify by terms such as *sensibility, good sense, sagacity, tact, insight*' (1989, 85; italics as in the source).

One ground for criticism of the category called 'aesthetic' has been that it was divorced from everyday utilitarian and ethical concerns. The details of aesthetic apprehension are a cultural project in itself. The objective of the discussion here is merely to clarify its relation to the political. A lot of contemporary discussion seems to collapse the two categories into each other. There are two versions of it. One, what are called aesthetic values are actually political values; the aesthetic is a euphemism for the political. Two, there might be something called the aesthetic. But it has been deployed to serve political ends. In *The Western Canon*, Harold Bloom responds to the first. Postcolonial response to Shakespeare being part of the empire-project belongs to the second category (Thank God Robert Clive did not write literary criticism!). As part of his narrative on the long chain of anxiety of influence in Western literature, Bloom objects to the exclusively political definition of literature coming from what he calls the School of Resentment: 'The cardinal principle of the current School of Resentment [is]: what is called aesthetic values emanates from class struggle' (1995, 23). According to Bloom, the argument that 'literary works join the Canon because of successful advertising and propaganda campaigns' is a case of 'academic radicalism' (20). The subtle aesthetic elitism of the statement notwithstanding, Bloom is well within his rights to object to the exclusively political definition of literature – which is the context of the assertion – coming from the 'School of Resentment' (Marxist, postcolonial, feminist and other similar schools of criticism). He is categorical that 'the deepest anxieties of literature are literary' (19). He rightly guesses the apprehension of political criticism vis-à-vis categories such as genius, masterpiece and aesthetic value. Bloom believes that the aesthetic quality of literary works can be ascertained regardless of who has written them and which social or ethnic group they hail from.[1] Bloom does provide a criterion for the canonicity of a work – 'strangeness': 'When you read a canonical work for a [sic] first time, you encounter a stranger, an uncanny startlement rather than a fulfillment of expectations' (3).

To return to our present discussion, the aesthetic and the political are mutually exclusive categories in a very special sense. As the discussion on delicate epistemes shows, it is a fluid realm where we have to be intuitively aware of subtle distinctions. Without any elitism which a Marxist or postcolonial critic is wary of, we can say that it requires a special ability, a non-reductive awareness of both the object and of our own evaluation. When we say that the aesthetic is political, unable to separate the fine grains of delicate truth, we are impatiently throwing off the container which holds the specimen. In other words, the act of developing exclusively political explanations for art is one wherein nuances can easily be lost. The objection of New Historicism to traditional criticism was that it viewed a literary work as an ahistorical, transcendent entity. Today we have reached the other extreme: texts are irretrievably buried in history and its politics that we have to be more careful gravediggers than those who buried Ophelia.

It is true that the category of the aesthetic has been invoked in several political proxy-discourses. One understands that in the past the discourse of literature itself was a sacrosanct discourse, and that this discourse had to do with relations of power. Nevertheless, that people who held power were arbitrators of what constitutes art and what we know under the label of art is the result of their arbitration does not necessarily prove that there is no such thing as the aesthetic. That the elite of the world was served by the handmaid of art is not an excuse to not study that maid's thoughts. The texts which are 'truly good' also might have a relation to the maintenance and perpetuation of power relations. In the exercise to clarify the aesthetic and the political, Eagleton's attempt, and that of political critics like him, is to understand the underlying dynamics of what we institutionally know as literature. Our attempt has been to understand the dynamics of what we often intuitively experience as literature.

If teaching Shakespeare was part of the empire-project, and if we still think his plays have enough merit in them to be studied, we can continue with him despite the political ends they served. Here we choose the aesthetic over the political. If we do away with him despite his merit, we do so on exclusively political grounds. If we think that he was an over-hyped mediocre playwright and we abandon him, we do so for aesthetic reasons. If we think that he was a mediocre playwright hyped by the discourse of the empire and we abandon him, we do so for aesthetic and political reasons. If we abandon him because there are other writers who are equally meritorious, it implies that the canon is too full, the curriculum too large and some writers will have to be dislodged from it.

Many instances where apolitical criticism was purportedly practised might have been deeply political. This does not mean that there can be no apolitical criticism. Apolitical criticism is possible not because we as readers or the texts as objects of study do not have politics. It is possible because when we consider the stanzaic structure of a poem, class-interests are largely irrelevant. Further, literatures whose entry into the canon is advocated on political grounds may not devote exclusive attention to political concerns though political criticism might expect the contrary, and this expectation might exert such a pressure on the writers. New writings might have new worlds, new experiences, new sensibilities and a new aesthetic to reveal, not merely 'resent' and 'resist' existing power-relations.

When one says that standards vary, it is not the same as saying that there are no standards. (We shall explore this question in the next section.) Then you ask me: 'Who decides the standards?' Then I reply: 'Substitute the "who" with a "what"'. Then you ask me: 'Who decides the "what"?' Then eager to avoid *reductio ad absurdum*, I say: Now that almost all ex cathedra pronouncements of the past have been successfully contested, let us pass the critical phase of the 'adolescent' struggle with the Eurocentric conservative elders (Matthew Arnold, for many) if we are to consider questions pertaining to literature in a balanced manner. As Graham Hough remarked half a century earlier, 'One cannot be very exhilarated by an outlook that consists mainly of automatic negations and routine nonconformities' (1964, 96).

4.2 What Is a Classic?

Etymologically, the English word 'classic' is derived from Latin *classicus*, which means 'belonging to a certain class', and historically came to mean 'of the highest class'. For centuries, a literary classic has been defined as a work which passes the test of time. It has been understood as a work of 'timeless quality', typified by Ben Jonson's posthumous and belated paean to Shakespeare: 'He was not for an age, but for all time' (1910). Though Jonson, by the way, also said of Shakespeare 'on this side idolatry [sic]' '*Sufflaminandus erat*' (he should have been clogged, or he needed restraint), he seems to have set the critical ball rolling, at least for modern literature, in this direction of defining a classic when he made the oft-quoted former statement. The temporal definition of a classic has two underlying assumptions. The first is that as time passes, readers will have thrown out a work of poor quality into the dustbin of literary history. This definition assumes time to be the matrix within which reflections occur on which works pass the test of quality and which do not. Though the criteria for a classic may change through centuries – Is there a classic under each genre? Can its delineation alter between the so-called high and low art? – these reflections need not involve a metalevel engagement of the criteria themselves. The second dimension is a more experiential one: every generation of readers is able to discover new significances in the work under question. Though the provenance of this rather traditional idea is different from that of deconstruction, the two share a striking similarity between them. As deconstruction has it, the text will renew itself across spaces and ages due to its 'textuality' (see our earlier discussion of iterability and relatability of texts to future worlds).

If the criterion of literary merit is test of time, we shall obviously miss the worth, if any, of contemporary works, which will be abandoned till a retrospective revaluation recovers them for the canon. For instance, it has been sixty years since Günter Grass's *The Tin Drum* arrived on the literary scene, and at least two generations of readers have arrived though not passed ever since. Is this long enough a period for literary evaluation? Strictly speaking, the so called test-of-time criterion is not a criterion at all. It does not provide us with the standards by which we can distinguish a classic from a work which is not one. It is rather a method, that too an indirect one, and hence the imperative to look for criteria elsewhere. Critical history has witnessed the emergence of many other methods and tests, which are equally elusive with regard to the criteria of literary excellence, Matthew Arnold's comparative 'touchstone' method being one (2009). The pervasive elusiveness is understandable given the fact that a consensus on 'literary value' is difficult to obtain. Ideological criticism of the literary canon, and of any professed criterion, is also premised on the near-impossibility of consensus. For instance, Terry Eagleton's historicizing narrative of the rise of literary studies as a discipline foregrounds the class- and racial basis of the apparently neutral definitions of literature [in the honorific sense]: 'The criteria of what counted as literature [...] were frankly ideological: writing which embodied the values and "tastes" of a particular social class qualified as literature, whereas a street ballad, a popular romance and perhaps even the drama did not' (1996, 15). The problem is that it is difficult to ascertain whether the criteria were *exclusively* ideological.

The lack of consensus, in turn, is also understandable since, as we discussed earlier in this chapter, and know experientially, apprehension of artistic value is a delicate process. The politico-cultural contexts and personal bases of the criteria notwithstanding, we cannot be held hostage either to relativism or to subjectivism. For that would render any discourse on the subject logically impossible. How can one evaluate a work without at least a vague understanding of the implied values or a reflection concerning our assumptions in this regard, particularly when even interpretations are conditioned by unconscious evaluations? Taking James Joyce's *Ulysses* as a test-case, I propose a re-examination of the criteria by which a work can be assessed as significant or otherwise. The same exercise can be repeated for Günter Grass's *The Tin Drum*, Gabriel Garcia Marquez's *One Hundred Years of Solitude* or any work for that matter. My endeavour will be to clarify criteria that we are intuitively aware of but have hesitated to articulate.

4.3 'Keep the Professors Busy for Centuries'

Ninety-seven years have passed since *Ulysses* was published as a book by Sylvia Beach's Shakespeare and Company (post its serialization in *The Little Review* and *The Egoist*), but it cannot be ascertained if a sufficient span of time has lapsed to apply the test-of-time method as could be and was done to its epic template, Homer's *Odyssey*. However, certain of its innate characteristics make it a highly probable winner if this is the method of testing. In his characteristic joco-serious style, Joyce told the French translator of *Ulysses*, Jacques Benoîst-Méchin: 'I've put in so many enigmas and puzzles that it will keep the professors busy for centuries arguing over what I meant, and that's the only way of insuring one's immortality' (Ellmann 1983, 521). That Joyce's insurance policy is still valid is clear enough, but the reasons thereof need some clarification. *Ulysses* is written at the micro-level and structured at the macro-level in a way that makes it capable of generating meanings at various levels, most of them beyond any assumed authorial intention. The book is an elaborate contrivance, an overstretched network of correspondences, motifs and symbols – a network capable of infinite expansion. As a result of this 'polymorphous capacity' (an allusion to Sigmund Freud's term 'polymorphous perversity'; in *Finnegans Wake*, it becomes a polyglottal perversity), at least four generations of readers have found in it new meanings, ideas and significances. All the *Ulysses*-criticism we have had in the last nine decades is a fragment of the book's hermeneutic infinity. For a simple instance, when Bloom's cat mews 'Mrkrgnao', it is not a meaningless sound or a random combination of letters. The Italian translator of the book has seen in 'Mrkrgnao' a covert version of 'Mrkr', the Greek spelling of Mercury, and thus a signal to the Homeric Hermes, the messenger from the gods (Levine 2004, 139).

The relatability of *Ulysses* as a text is apparently (only apparently) compromised by the self-professed hermetic tendency of avant-garde modernism. In the same vein, its unapologetic subject matter – the ordinary and the commonplace – finds itself, paradoxically, at odds with this tendency. The self-reflexive difficulty of modernist texts has been discussed for almost a century. The difficulty of Joyce's later texts, *Ulysses* and *Finnegans Wake*, seems to stem from two textual characteristics. First, their reading requires a fairly large cultural repertoire (linguistic as well, in the case of the *Wake*) and mythico-historical memory, which is ordinarily not possible for the reader to achieve. *Ulysses* self-reflexively alludes to the challenges posed by its telegraphic allusiveness when it has Malachi Mulligan, who appears in the very first episode of the book, wittily mention, in a veiled reference to Yeats and the texts of the Celtic revival, the 'five lines of text and ten pages of notes about the folk and fish gods of Dundrum' (Joyce 1984, 1.365–67). Second, it is the question of why certain elements are there in the textual space, after all. Why should seven pages of the book be spent on Bloom's defecation, which happens in full view of the reader? Across generations Joyce's insistence on the undistinguished aspects of everyday life has exhilarated many readers and baffled or disappointed many others. While the shared character of the quotidian activities invited many to a vicarious participation, the apparent absence of a narrative rationale behind them guided the irritation of many early readers. Carl Gustav Jung was disappointed that 'nothing happen[ed]' in the 735 pages of the book: 'Every sentence raises an expectation which is not fulfilled; finally, out of sheer resignation, you come to expect nothing any longer' (1970, 584–85).

The discussion pertaining to the status of *Ulysses* as a classic needs to factor in the complex, and the seemingly convoluted, relationship that modernism has with *profanum vulgus*. Indeed the 'difficult' art of the modernists, including Joyce, places itself beyond the reach of the common reader, an attitude expressed by Eugene Jolas in his pronouncement in the Paris-based journal *Transition*, 'The plain reader be damned' (Ellmann 1983, 588n). According to Malcolm Bradbury and James McFarlane, modernist art represents 'a hoarding of the artistic powers against the populace' (1976, 28). But this distanciation has an objective and is to be seen in the context of the avant-garde's negative engagement with reality. As Theodor Adorno argues in *Aesthetic Theory*, it is precisely by a critical distancing from the masses and the existing reality that modernism is able to critique both and conceive a new reality. That is why Adorno claims that modernist art respects masses by showing them what they can be 'rather than adapting to their dehumanized condition' (1984, 341). Adorno defends modernist art's tendency of cordoning itself off from the populace. According to him, art that is truly emancipative does not reflect on and communicate with society. Rather, it resists society: 'Art is the negative knowledge of the actual world' (1977, 160). Realist art that caters to the masses faces the danger of integration into the dynamics of the system. Art as social protest faces the threat of degenerating into an affirmation of the status quo. Society is willing to incorporate protests and assert its own totalizing power. Adorno sees this totalizing power in the 'culture industry' (Horkheimer and Adorno 2002, 94–136). The term 'culture industry' denotes the manner in which contemporary capitalist society accommodates artistic practices, even those which were once radical, into its own processes of commercialism and commoditization. To Adorno, the ideal art is a hermetic one. The irony, however, is that the very character of Joyce's avant-garde art as an esoteric system makes it a commodity of a different order – a collector's item, with a heightened market value.[2]

Just as the book's esoteric potential for meaning-generation enhances its value when tested by the temporal method, the reverse can also be true with regard to the passage of time. The expansion of the canon has rendered the erstwhile distinction between the so-called high and low literature more or less invalid. As we know, contemporary academic research devotes an unprecedented degree of attention to popular culture. Folk tales and folk arts, street theatre, advertisements, travel and cookery books and graphic novels are legitimate critical concerns. Technological changes have ushered in research on cinema, cyber punk, print and television media, social media and e-novels. Do old definitions of canons and classics still hold water? Despite its early characterization as 'high art' and its reputation as an esoteric work, *Ulysses*, like the rest of Joyce's oeuvre, being replete with pantomimes, folk songs, musichall numbers, street and barroom ballads, bits of popular fiction, advertisement jingles, nursery rhymes and, above all, bawdy Irish jokes, has a strong basis in popular culture.[3] Understandably, Joyce has somehow managed to transcend the high-low distinction and the related cultural transitions. In fact, contemporary popular culture has a Joyce buzz. Joyce is the subject of a lot of popular intertextuality, Frank Costello (Jack Nicholson)'s 'non serviam' quote and young Colin's immediate identification of the source in Martin Scorsese's *The Departed* (2006) and the Joycean associations of the Soviet code-name Ulysses/Stas Siyanko (Oleg Stefan) in Robert De Niro's *The Good Shepherd* (2006) being notable examples. Ironic as it might seem of a work which critiques mass marketing and commodity capitalism from the inside (Bloom is an advertising canvasser), as Emer Nolan points out, 'in Ireland, quotations from Joyce's texts have been used to sell all kinds of commodities, from lemon soap [Bloom buys it from a Dublin chemist] to sausages' (2007, 153). *Ulysses* has something for everybody. I am reminded of an observation made by a student the last time I taught the text: 'Reading *Ulysses* is like being in a supermarket. You don't know what to take and what to leave'. As for myself, when I see the flag of the European Union fluttering over the chateau of William the Conqueror in Caen, I wonder what Joyce, with his humorous critique of parochial Irish nationalism, would have thought. Nevertheless, there are dimensions of a text in respect of which *Ulysses* might have lost its sheen in course of time. As noted earlier, it is doubtful whether an allusive text such as this may have as much impact in the age of the internet as high modernist ones had had. Technology changes the text-reader symmetry!

4.4 A Milestone Approach

Though difficulty stimulates exegetical research, it cannot be the sole reason for perpetuation of interest. My contention is that a work needs to be considered significant or insignificant not because it passes or does not pass the test of time, but because it engages substantial political, cultural, social, philosophical and aesthetic questions. The claim of *Ulysses* to the status of a classic rests not on its passing the temporal test but on its ability to engage such questions. Perhaps, it may pass the former because it fulfils the latter requirement or expectation. Many projects, both aesthetic and sociopolitical, are at work in Joyce's texts and, not surprisingly, they have been at the centre of many perennial concerns, quests, re-examinations and dilemmas.

During the early decades of Joyce criticism, the mundane events that Joyce consciously chose to depict in *Ulysses* at the expense of conventional narrative expectations were read in conjunction with the catastrophe of the Great War as symptomatic of the absurdity of contemporary life, a mild prelude to the Beckettian Absurd. In the Literature of the Absurd, human action is represented as fundamentally pointless in a universe deprived of its metaphysical moorings. Beckettian absurd is, of course, not the reappearance of the ordinary as the ordinary. Here the ordinary is short-circuited back into negative metaphysical significances. Coming as they did in the wake of the first war fought on a global scale, and the fragmentation and alienation in daily life wrought by a dehumanizing capitalist production, they were bound to receive such pessimistic but significant appraisals. To T. S. Eliot, who otherwise commended *Ulysses*, the life in the book pointed to 'the immense panorama of futility and anarchy which [was] contemporary history'. He believed that in order to give 'a shape and a significance' (1970, 270) to this deplorable state of affairs, Joyce and many writers who would follow him were obliged to pursue 'the mythical method'. Similarly, Jean Paris saw the triviality of Joyce's content as a sign of degeneration from the ideals of the past and atrophy of the times when *Ulysses* was written (qtd. in Lobsien 1978, 20).[4] Erich Auerbach also saw the phenomenon in a pessimistic light, as 'a mirror of the decline of our world' (1953, 551). To him, the book presents an 'atmosphere of universal doom', 'confusion and helplessness' and a 'blatant and painful cynicism' (551). In fact, that the book reflected the spirit of its time (*Zeitgeist*) was so taken for granted that when the belief was belied it resulted in sharp responses. For instance, Marxist critic Karl Radek complained about Joyce's neglect of momentous historical developments. He found Joyce's 'method' at the most suitable 'for describing petty, insignificant, trivial people, their actions, thoughts and feelings'. It would, Radek observed, prove 'utterly worthless if the author were to approach [...] the great events of the class struggle, the titanic clashes of the modern world' (1970, 625).

Joyce has been cited by almost every major thinker and critic of the last one hundred years for one purpose or the other. For instance, Charles Taylor, perhaps the greatest philosopher alive, exploring the making of the modern identity in *Sources of the Self: The Making of the Modern Identity* (1989), employs Joyce's concept of epiphany, in relation to affirmation of ordinary life. Martha Nussbaum, a philosopher who can be called a public intellectual, in her book *Upheavals of Thought: The Intelligence of Emotions* (2001), considers Bloom, the tolerant cuckold, a political model for our times (679–714). Bloom's conscious decision to abstain himself from home during the rendezvous between Molly and Boylan illustrates a philosophy of the other: a You-relation, which recognizes the subjectivity of the other as another I, in contradistinction to an It-relation, which merely objectifies and uses the other – a distinction made by philosopher Martin Buber. Similarly, Declan Kiberd's book *Ulysses and Us: The Art of Everyday Life in Joyce's Masterpiece* (2009) argues that contrary to its reputation as an obscure text, *Ulysses* makes available to common man the wisdom and art of ordinary life. Similarly, in a case of analogous reasoning, Fredric Jameson claims in *Marxism and Form* (1971) that *Ulysses* is structured in a way that replicates the totalizing dynamics of capitalism. M. Keith Booker's *Ulysses, Capitalism, and Colonialism: Reading Joyce after the Cold War* (2000) is another example which shows the book's ability proleptically to engage phenomena beyond the period of its origin. The point is that writing on Joyce is not mere literary criticism. The conclusion one can draw from the proliferating examples of the above-mentioned kind across disciplinary boundaries is that Joyce is not merely a creative writer who extended the frontiers of fiction with his experimental writings but one who is an indispensable part of humanity's long endeavour to understand itself. I am aware that terms such as 'humanity' and 'human nature' are suspect in the contemporary critical climate. But in order to understand a phenomenon, one has to suspend for a while the uncompromising conceptual scepticism and the assumed naiveté which accompanies this scepticism. In any case, Joyce's works have been milestones in Western cultural history, both reflecting and triggering the evolution of the Occidental world view in the twentieth century.

In an essay entitled 'Joyce à la Braudel: The Long-Temporality of *Ulysses*' (2013), I have argued that Joyce espouses alternative historical trajectories neglected by traditional historiographic paradigms, which largely deal with great personages and momentous events. The essay draws a parallel between the quotidian material life depicted in *Ulysses* and the concept of 'structural history' proposed by the French micro-historian Fernand Braudel.[5] In *Ulysses*, Joyce foregrounds the historicity of the quotidian and holds out the down-to-earth praxis, the immediate challenges and possible fulfilment in the daily life of ordinary men and women as an experiential contrast to a 'grand history' of conspicuous (and cataclysmic) events. If one historicizes the everyday Joyce, this contrastive grand history may be seen to have comprised of not only the Great War but also the seven-century-long English imperial rule in Ireland, the climactic years of the violent Irish struggle for independence, the civil war that followed and various kinds of religious and sectarian bigotry, including anti-Semitism, both in Ireland and on the Continent, where Joyce was in voluntary exile. Paradoxically, it is the historiographically privileged phenomena of the greater world – wars, civil wars, colonial domination, violent nationalism and anti-Semitism – that constitute the content of the 'nightmare [of history] from which' Stephen is 'trying to awake' (1984, 2.377).

Indeed Joyce's greatest contribution has been in the understanding of everyday life, its unconcealed subtleties and unarticulated intricacies. No doubt the quotidian in *Ulysses* is historically specific, set at the beginning of the twentieth century in urban Dublin. It is not even an Irish quotidian. Joyce knew very little about the Irish countryside. Further, within Dublin, it is only the lower middle class that finds space in the book. Except for indirect references, the urban working class represented in Seán O'Casey's plays and the rural folk in John Millington Synge's works are conspicuous by absence in *Ulysses*. The life experiences of a specific group of people at a specific moment in time cannot claim universal significance. Having said this, it would be equally naive to consider a cosmopolitan writer's representation of life as only locally or nationally relevant. One of Joyce's attempts as he moved from *Dubliners* (1914) to *Finnegans Wake* (1939) was to impart a transnational and transtemporal significance to his works. The *Wake* presents the cosmic dream of an archetypal man HCE (Here Comes Everybody/Humphrey Chimpden Earwicker). In *Ulysses* Joyce makes Bloom's day so representative that many of its aspects will have implications that transcend time and place. He told Arthur Power, 'I always write about Dublin, because if I can get to the heart of Dublin I can get to the heart of all the cities of the world. In the particular is contained the universal' (Ellmann1983, 505). Acknowledging Joyce's ability to capture the universal in the particular, Herman Broch, one of the first Jews who received Joyce's help during the *Anschluss* to escape from German territory, refers to 16 June 1904 as the '*Welt-Alltag der Epoche* [universal quotidian]' (1975, 64). Virtually every aspect of the spectrum of existence – education, work, leisure, shopping, sleep, family, birth, sex, death, social camaraderie, religion, politics and art – finds a place in the encyclopaedic novel. Its representative inclusiveness makes Bloomsday a microcosmic specimen where the workings of human life are instantiated.

That Joyce raises the ordinary and the commonplace to the sanctity of religion and ritual is vouchsafed by his use, in *Stephen Hero*, of the term 'epiphany' to describe its trivia. *A Portrait of the Artist as a Young Man*, a revised version of the partially extant *Stephen Hero*, opens with Stephen's vivid recollection of the story about the 'moocow', which his father told him. He remembers the physical sensations of infancy with immediacy – the smell of his parents and the change from warmth to cold when he wets the bed (1977, 7). He is attentive to the sound 'suck' produced by dirty water going down through the hole in the basin (11). In *Ulysses* the odour of the pickings of his toe nail, nauseating though it may seem to the reader, takes Bloom back in time to childhood (1984, 17.1488–96). The tender sense that Joyce's detailed portrait of Bloom leaves is that of a little, finite life: Here was a man, uncounted and isolated, who passes unnoticed, through or alongside the otherwise convivial Dublin gatherings. Here was a man with a mole on his nose. And one day he ceased to be. That Rudolf Bloom, Leopold's father, had purchased 'a new boater straw hat' (17.629–32) before his suicide speaks volumes about his inner life, which contrasts with the matter-of-fact manner in which Joyce makes Bloom recollect the scene of the inquest. The lamb wool corselet that Molly knitted for her infant son, Rudy, and with which she buried him (14.269) and the bowl of china into which Stephen's mother vomited the bile in her deathbed (1.108–10) are experiential tokens of a life that is unknown, of an unaccounted history. Small things of ordinary human life matter because they are *framed by mortality*. The finitude of life imparts an existential momentousness and an emotional gravity to non-events. When people are gone, these small things attain an unprecedented significance by 'retrospective arrangement', a repeated phrase in *Ulysses*. The strength of literature lies in its ability – a sensitive audacity – to deal with such delicate reality. To a world of instant generalizations and quick dismissals, where words have failed to signify, where habitual scepticism is mistaken for critical intelligence, literature such as this seems to be suggesting that all knowledge is a matter of delicate epistemes.

Virginia Woolf, another writer of interior monologues, praised Joyce as a 'spiritual' writer for his ability to understand the interiority of being (1968, 190). Joyce's own interior monologues lay bare before the reader the subtle realities of his characters' inner life – even semi-formed and half-articulated thoughts, dubious perceptions, overwhelming feelings and unconventional opinions. To this end Joyce fragmented his narratives, recast English, perverted its syntax, broke down its vocabulary, peeped into its semantic possibilities and in the process rendered the Oxford English Dictionary irreversibly obsolete.

At another level, the self-conscious representation of trivia in *Ulysses* is also meta-art. Therefore, it is possible to detect in it a metalevel significance as well. One may account for the presence of elements such as Bloom's defecation by arguing that by incorporating inconspicuous occurrences, the author is raising a meta-literary question: 'What will count as literature?' The Joycean trivia may be seen as part of the transgressive avant-garde response to the arbitrariness of defining and delimiting art.[6] Joyce's fiction does reveal the arbitrariness of unwritten literary norms through their breach. In the 'Calypso' episode Bloom defecates and wipes himself with a copy of *Titbits*, where the prize story of 'Matcham's Masterstroke' by Philip Beaufoy has appeared. Material that is conventionally unacceptable as art and frowned upon is self-reflexively brought in contact with the printed word.

Ulysses has also been a paradigmatic text for many schools of criticism. We have discussed one of them, genetic criticism, in detail. Similarly, geocriticism is a contemporary critical approach that aims to study real and fictional geographical spaces, its chief practitioners being Bertrand Westphal and Robert Tally. Perhaps, the single source of origin for modern geocriticism is spatial studies of Joyce's Dublin. When Joyce told Frank Budgen that he 'want[ed] to give a picture of Dublin so complete that if the city suddenly disappeared from the earth it could be reconstructed out of [his] book' (Budgen 1960, 69), he was setting, albeit joco-seriously, new standards of spatial correctness in fiction. Budgen adds: 'Joyce wrote the "Wandering Rocks" episode with a map of Dublin before him on which were traced in red ink the paths of the Earl of Dudley and Father Conmee whose journeys frame the occurrences of the episode. He calculated to a minute the time necessary for his characters to cover a given distance of the city' (124). Another school known as the New Economic Criticism explores 'parallels and analogies between linguistic and economic systems', 'between language and money' (Woodmansee and Osteen 1999, 14–15). Mark Osteen's economic analysis of *Ulysses* views Joyce's significatory practice itself as characterized by an economy of thrift and extravagance (1995, 200). Such an endeavour is valid because literary studies follow an analogous mode of reasoning.

One of the trends in Joyce Criticism in the last forty odd years has been a political radicalization of his writings (e.g., Enda Duffy's *Subaltern Ulysses*). Such an approach enables us to assess the extent and meaning of the subtle 'commitment' of a writer who *was* widely believed to have cultivated the image of a detached aesthete, primarily interested in form and technique. As Joyce's position on Irish nationalism demonstrates, lack of ideological commitment does not necessarily mean lack of interest. We have seen in the course of our discussion that he is vitally interested in everything under the sun but engages things in a way that suits his art. Only we have to decipher the nature of this engagement in the book's maze of fragmentary references, its jarring aesthetic, serio-comic play, undermining parody and ubiquitous irony. A tenacious exercise on these lines can hopefully illustrate what a classic actually means.

In a very limited sense, we may call Joyce's writing 'aphilosophical'. Here everything is valid; nothing has absolute authority. The texts are a play of competing discourses, world views and lifestyles, even the most aberrant ones. Of course, some are singled out for parody – ecclesiastical tyranny and parochial nationalism, for instance. But one cannot hierarchize the various discourses and enlist the author as the ideologue of a cause or the mouthpiece of an idea. This makes Joyce, paradoxically, the high priest of mismatches and contaminations.

4.5 Ever-Changing Domains of Knowledge

Today it might sound a truism to claim that domains of knowledge are not metaphysically stable entities but subject to inevitable historical change. Changes in the domain of knowledge are not merely due to the temporal character of knowledge-advances – the progressive results of explorations, discoveries, theorizations and what Thomas Kuhn (1996) calls 'paradigm shifts'. Historically, the legitimacy of knowledge depended more on power and ideology than on intrinsic worth. Michel Foucault's term *episteme* (historical a priori) denotes historically specific norms of discourse that determine what can be accepted as valid knowledge. As a result of historical–ideological scrutiny, disciplines have become self-conscious today. Perhaps, there is no better example of this disciplinary self-consciousness than the sophisticated and effervescent debate which problematizes the subject matter of literary studies – notions of what qualifies as 'literature'.

The dynamic character of knowledge has enabled several previously excluded social and ethnic groups to have their concerns accepted as legitimate academic subject-matter. The writings of African Americans, native Americans and Australian Aborigines have won their place in the literary canon. Many areas of study have emerged on the world literary scene, for example, Queer theory and Dalit literature. Similarly, feminist theory has helped recognize a previously unrecognized corpus of writing by women authors, interpret the plight of women as that of a doubly colonized group and subvert gender stereotypes. The postcolonial counter-discourse has helped re-examine the literary canon and reconfigure the international literary landscape by contesting and dismantling ontological assumptions underlying the Western canon and creating a legitimate place for the new 'englishes' and literatures written in them. It has successfully taken up questions of literary value and judgment by deconstructing received canonical norms from a decolonizing position. What were deemed universal values have been revealed to be historically and culturally specific. This development also helped writers recognize that their worlds were 'literary enough'.

With the expansion of the literary canon, the erstwhile distinction between 'high' and 'low' forms of literary art is no longer considered valid. Though etymologically, the word 'literature' is applied only to written texts, oral texts and performances are also being studied. The word 'orature' was coined by the Ugandan scholar Pio Zirimu to cover earlier exceptions. Another development has been the expansion of literary texts to include diverse cultural practices of societies and their meanings, under the purview of what has come to be called literary and cultural studies. As the result of New Historicist rethinking, texts have also been successfully *opened to history*. They are discussed in 'culturally relativistic' ways. The critical tools and conceptual frameworks of comparatively recent disciplines such as cultural studies have also facilitated the study of several everyday concerns (e.g., spatial politics of rural communities).

Many proponents of the new literatures in English also emphasize the need for indigenous theories and native critical tools to grapple adequately with the cultural complexities and aesthetic nuances of the texts. The plea for a hermeneutic based on native literary traditions is based on the assumption that these literatures represent an indigenous aesthetic sensibility rather than an English or European one. For example, in India, some literary critics contend that the critical repertoire of ancient treatises such as *Natyashastra*, consisting of concepts such as *rasa* (emotion) and *dhvani* (suggestion) are more relevant and suitable than 'imported' ones for appreciation and interpretation of contemporary Indian works, in vernacular languages and in English.

The democratization of knowledge, as illustrated by literary studies, outlined above, is a reflective analogue of the historical progress, its limitations notwithstanding, of democracy – a movement from the few to the many and to all. If one is ready to accept that knowledge can detach itself from the totalizing logic of power, it can even serve as an anticipative analogue. Indeed, from a democratic perspective, contestation and inclusion are welcome in the domain of knowledge. But the development is not without its pitfalls. It is argued in many erstwhile colonies that Shakespeare (and several other canonical writers) was a phenomenon overrated as part of the empire-project and must be replaced or at least supplemented by native authors. The plea is: 'Why study alien phenomena? Why not study *our own* literature?' Remember that what is our own and what is alien itself is a delicate matter and often based on contestable categories such as 'national literature'. The human consciousness is so receptive that it chooses inputs it needs for its growth regardless of the source of the input. The flipside of this 'nativist apologetics' is that knowledge gets ghettoized on national, regional, sub-regional and other sociological grounds. Let us not so fragment knowledge on sociological lines that a Dalit student will come to think himself capable of researching only on Dalit literature, a tribal student exclusively studies oral texts and so on. That would be a travesty of the original democratic inclusiveness of knowledge and lead to an inadvertent exclusivism.

4.6 Negotiated Possibilities

One of my concerns in this book has been the connections between the academic and the experiential. Therefore, let me end on a quotidian note. We return home after a day's work and watch a television commercial which captures all the beauty and magic we have longed for. In the heart of our hearts we know that this beauty and magic are a possibility that is available right in the middle of our own lives, that we do not have to buy the product that is advertised to access the beauty and magic, that it is an advertising strategy to make us think otherwise. The artful commercial has nonetheless encapsulated these for us in a transient, dreamy, imaginative instant and one gains one's quotidian energies from it. We watch the climax of a well-made movie accompanied by a musical score which evokes in us a sense of the sublime. Our thoughts, emotions and experience get organized around the template provided by the scene. Our sense of life is raised to a high pitch of glorious significance. Yet, we know that it is the enactment of an audio-visual formula, circulation of tropes tested for their psychological efficacy and financed by a clever producer. We listen to a televangelist who utters words which touch our hearts, engender in us a 'kingdom of God is within you feel', answer to our concerns about our posterity and assures us that there is a covenant between Him and us, between Him and our generations to come, that He shall remember our supplications when He walketh the earth long after we are gone. But we know that this is smart talk, a rhetorically efficacious performance that knows its audience.

The paradox of existence is that many of its aspects that are resisted as commercial, ideological and power-driven are also its props and mainstays.

Religion, popular culture, collective beliefs, commodities and familial and gender relations – the human world and its texts – exhibit this paradox. For instance, education, a process of ideological conditioning, is, as Raymond Williams puts it, 'the process of giving to the ordinary members of society its full common meanings, and the skills that enable them to amend these meanings, in the light of their personal and common experience' (1989, 14). A possible response to the paradox is a productively oxymoronic approach of diligent negotiation, by which one can make use of what one is offered as resources of life while understanding its true nature. Be sceptically nourished! It is an ironic logic of creative utilization and supersession (Hegelian *Aufhebung*), not of repudiation or negation. While making the case for resistance and subversion, it also needs to be admitted that confining the agenda of life to ideological resistance only impoverishes life in its processes of making and remaking. If human existence has to be a true poiēses, it has to transcend this exclusive logic. A hermeneutic of suspicion uncomplemented by that of possibilities is unconducive to it. A hermeneutic of possibilities envisages a give and take with the given, a practical logic of creative reception and productive re-employment. Harmonizing the two hermeneutics involves shifts between the positions of a critic and a practitioner of life. The alternative would be what one may call a cultural fatalism.

Notes

1 Literary studies seem to be in the grip of what may be called a 'versus fixation'. Critics are accustomed to pitting one entity against another – race against race, the East against the West, man against woman and so on. I have deliberately used the Freudian term 'fixation'. Psychoanalysis defines fixation as an inability to resolve the conflicts of one phase of psychosexual development (psychosocial development for Erik Erikson) and proceed to another. The individual gets stuck in a phase. I consider contestation to be a necessary but insufficient phase in the arduous task of understanding.
2 For a further discussion of the economic logic of modernism, see Lawrence Rainey, 'The Cultural Economy of Modernism', *The Cambridge Companion to Modernism*, pp. 33–69.
3 See Richard Brandon Kershner, *Joyce and Popular Culture* (Gainesville: University Press of Florida, 1996).
4 Paris says, 'Wenn die »Odyssee« hier in entarteter Form auflebt, so nur, weil unsere Welt nicht mehr die Kraft besitzt, eine zweite zu schaffen, weil ihre Kultur bereits dazu verurteilt ist, sich an Abfällen zu sättigen [If the *Odyssey* revives here in degenerated form, and only thus, it is because our world no more possesses the strength to create a second one, because her culture is already condemned to feed itself on rubbish]' (qtd. in Lobsien 1978, 20).
5 The cataclysmic historical events which precipitated the crisis-ridden world view of avant-garde modernism also led to innovative historical inquiries. One call for historical rethinking came from Fernand Braudel, who belonged to what has become known

as the Annales School of historians. See note 4 in Chapter 1 for a discussion of Braudel and the Annales School.

6   We would do well to remember that the Dadaists had hoped, by destruction of canons of taste and of logic, to show their contempt for bourgeois society. They had made Zürich their home like Joyce, and he was aware of their programme. Tom Stoppard presents a fictional meeting between Joyce and the Dadaist poet Tristan Tzara in his comedy *Travesties* (1974).

REFERENCES

Abrams, M. H. 1989. *Doing Things with Texts: Essays in Criticism and Critical Theory*. Edited by Michael Fisher. New York: Norton.
Adorno, Theodor W. 1977. 'Reconciliation under Duress'. In *Aesthetics and Politics*, edited by Ernst Bloch, translated by Rodney Livingstone, 151–76. London: NLB.
———. 1984. *Aesthetic Theory*. Translated by C. Lenhardt, edited by Gretel Adorno and Rolf Tiedemann. London: Routledge.
Althusser, Louis. 1971. 'Ideology and Ideological State Apparatuses'. In *Lenin and Philosophy and Other Essays*, translated by Ben Brewster, 127–86. New York: Monthly Review Press.
Aristotle. 1920. *The Poetics*. Translated by Ingram Bywater. Oxford: Clarendon Press. Project Gutenberg. Accessed on 20 November 2012. http://www.gutenberg.org/files/6763/6763-h/6763- h.htm.
———. 2000. *Aristotle: Nichomachean Ethics*. Translated by Roger Crisp. Cambridge: Cambridge University Press.
Armstrong, Karen. 1999. *A History of God. From Abraham to the Present: The 4000-Year Quest for God*. London: Vintage.
Arnold, Matthew. 2009. *Study of Poetry*. Poetry Foundation. Accessed on 31 August 2019. https://www.poetryfoundation.org/articles/69374/the-study-of-poetry.
Attridge, Derek. 2000. *Joyce Effects: On Language, Theory, and History*. Cambridge: Cambridge University Press.
Auerbach, Erich. 1953. *Mimesis: The Representation of Reality in Western Literature*. Translated by Willard R. Trask. Princeton, NJ: Princeton University Press.
Barthes, Roland. 1972. *Mythologies*. Translated by Annette Lavers. London: Cape.
———. 1977. 'From Work to Text'. In *Image, Music*, Text, translated by Stephen Heath. New York: Hill and Wang.
Beckett, Samuel. [1929] 1972. *Our Exagmination Round His Factification for Incamination of Work in Progress*. London: Faber and Faber.
Beja, Morris. 1971. *Epiphany in the Modern Novel*. Seattle, WA: University of Washington Press.
Bennington, Geoffrey. 1993. 'Derridabase'. In *Jacques Derrida*, edited by Geoffrey Bennington and Jacques Derrida, translated by Geoffrey Bennington, 3–316. Chicago, IL: University of Chicago Press.
Bloch, Ernst. 1986. *The Principle of Hope*. 3 vols. Translated by Neville Plaice, Stephen Plaice and Paul Knight. Cambridge, MA: MIT Press.
Bloom, Harold. 1995. *The Western Canon: The Books and School of the Ages*. London: Macmillan.
Booker, M. Keith. 2000. *Ulysses, Capitalism, and Colonialism: Reading Joyce after the Cold War*. Westport, CT: Greenwood Press.
Borah, Anupom, and K. P. Mohanakumar. 2009. 'Melatonin Inhibits L-DOPA Induced 6-OHDA'. *Journal of Pineal Research* 47: 293–300.

Bradbury, Malcolm, and James McFarlane, eds. 1976. *Modernism 1890–1930*. Harmondsworth: Penguin.
Braudel, Fernand. 1980. *On History*. Translated by Sarah Matthews. Chicago, IL: University of Chicago Press.
———. 1981. *The Structures of Everyday Life: The Limits of the Possible*. Translated by Siân Reynolds. Vol. 1 of *Civilization and Capitalism 15th–18th Century*. 3 vols. London: Collins.
———. 1992. *The Mediterranean and the Mediterranean World in the Age of Philip II*. Translated by Siân Reynolds. New York: Harper.
Brecht, Bertolt. 1964. *Brecht on Theatre: The Development of an Aesthetic*. Edited and translated by John Willett. New York: Hill and Wang.
Broch, Hermann. 1975. 'James Joyce und die Gegenwart'. In *Hermann Broch: Schriften zur Literatur* 1, edited by Paul Michael Lützeler, 63–94. Frankfurt am Main: Suhrkamp.
Brunsdale, Mitzi M. 1993. *James Joyce: A Study of the Short Fiction*. Twayne's Studies in Short Fiction Series 45. New York: Twayne.
Buber, Martin. 1970. *I and Thou: A New Translation with a Prologue 'I and You' and Notes by Walter Kaufmann*. Translated by Walter Kaufmann. New York: Scribner's.
Budgen, Frank. 1960. *James Joyce and the Making of Ulysses*. Bloomington, IN: Indiana University Press.
Bulson, Eric. 2006. *The Cambridge Introduction to James Joyce*. Cambridge: Cambridge University Press.
Cornell, Drucilla. 1992. *The Philosophy of the Limit*. New York: Routledge.
Davies, Tony. 1997. *Humanism*. London: Routledge.
de Biasi, Pierre-Marc. 2004. 'Toward a Science of Literature: Manuscript Analysis and the Genesis of the Work'. In *Genetic Criticism: Texts and Avant-Textes*, edited by Jed Deppman, Daniel Ferrer and Michael Groden, 36–68. Philadelphia, PA: University of Pennsylvania Press.
De Man, Paul. 1974. 'Nietzsche's Theory of Rhetoric'. *Symposium* 28: 33–51.
Deppman, Jed, Daniel Ferrer and Michael Groden, ed. 2004. *Genetic Criticism: Texts and Avant-Textes*. Philadelphia, PA: University of Pennsylvania Press.
Derrida, Jacques. 1972. 'Structure, Sign, and Play in the Discourse of the Human Sciences'. In *The Structuralist Controversy*, edited by Richard Macksey and Eugenio Donato, 247–72. Baltimore, MD: John Hopkins University Press.
———. 1978. *Writing and Difference*. Translated by Alan Bass. London: RKP.
———. 1981. *Dissemination*. Translated by Barbara Johnson. Chicago, IL: University of Chicago Press.
———. 1982. 'Signature Event Context'. In *Margins of Philosophy*, translated by Alan Bass, 307–30. Chicago, IL: University of Chicago Press.
———. 1983. 'The Time of a Thesis: Punctuations'. In *Philosophy in France Today*, edited by Alan Montefiore, translated by Kathleen McLaughlin, 34–51. Cambridge: Cambridge University Press.
———. 1984. 'Two Words for Joyce'. In *Post-Structuralist Joyce: Essays from the French*, edited by Derek Attridge and Daniel Ferrer, translated by Geoff Bennington, 145–59. Cambridge: Cambridge University Press.
———. 1991. 'Ulysses Gramophone: Hear Say Yes in Joyce'. In *A Derrida Reader: Between the Blinds*, edited by Peggy Kamuf, 569–99. New York: Columbia University Press.
———. 1995. 'The Time Is Out of Joint'. In *Deconstruction Is/in America: A New Sense of the Political*, edited by Anselm Haverkamp, translated by Peggy Kamuf, 14–41. New York: New York University Press.

Duffy, Enda. 1994. *The Subaltern Ulysses*. Minneapolis: University of Minnesota Press.
Eagleton, Terry. 1990. *The Ideology of the Aesthetic*. Oxford, MN: Basil Blackwell.
———. 1996. *Literary Theory: An Introduction*. 2nd ed. Malden, MA: Blackwell.
Eldridge, Richard. 2010. 'Truth in Poetry: Particulars and Universals'. In *A Companion to the Philosophy of Literature*, edited by Garry L. Hagberg and Walter Jost, 385–98. Malden, MA: Wiley-Blackwell.
Eliade, Mircea. 1954. *The Myth of the Eternal Return, or Cosmos and History*. Translated by Willard R. Trask. Princeton, NJ: Princeton University Press.
Eliot, T. S. 1921. *The Sacred Wood: Essays on Poetry and Criticism*. New York: Knopf.
———. 1970. '*Ulysses*, Order and Myth'. In *James Joyce: The Critical Heritage*, edited by Robert H. Deming, 268–71. London: Routledge.
Ellis, John M. 1989. *Against Deconstruction*. Princeton, NJ: Princeton University Press.
Ellmann, Richard. 1983. *James Joyce*. Rev. ed. New York: Oxford University Press.
Fish, Stanley. 1980. *Is There a Text in This Class?: The Authority of Interpretive Communities*. Cambridge, MA: Harvard University Press.
Fiske, Susan T., and Shelley E. Taylor. 2013. *Social Cognition: From Brains to Culture*. London: Sage.
Forrest Gump. 1994. Dir. Robert Zemeckis. USA: Wendy Finerman. Pramount Pictures. Film.
Foucault, Michel. 1970. *The Order of Things: An Archaeology of the Human Sciences*. London: Tavistock.
Frankl, Viktor. 1992. *Man's Search for Meaning: An Introduction to Logotherapy*. Boston, MA: Beacon Press.
Freud, Sigmund. 2003. *The Uncanny*. Translated by David McLintock. London: Penguin.
Frye, Northrop. 1957. *Anatomy of Criticism: Four Essays*. Princeton, NJ: Princeton University Press.
Gabler, Hans Walter. 2008. Centrality of the Text in Joyce Studies. University College Dublin. Global Irish Research Institute, Dublin. 17 April 2008. James Joyce Research Colloquium. Keynote Address.
Gasché, Rodolphe. 1994. *Inventions of Difference: On Jacques Derrida*. Cambridge, MA: Harvard University Press.
Genette, Gérard. 1980. *Palimpsests: Literature in the Second Degree*. Translated by Channa Newman and Claude Doubinsky. Lincoln, NE: University of Nebraska Press.
Genette, Raymond Debray. 2004. 'Flaubert's "A Simple Heart", or How to Make an Ending'. In *Genetic Criticism: Texts and Avant-Textes*, edited by Jed Deppman, Daniel Ferrer and Michael Groden, 69–95. Philadelphia, PA: University of Pennsylvania Press.
George, Jibu Mathew. 2010. 'Further Explorations in the Philosophy of the Other in Relation to Extreme Experience'. *Indian Philosophical Quarterly* 37, no.1–4: 109–31.
———. 2013. 'Joyce à la Braudel: The Long-Temporality of *Ulysses*'. *KronoScope: Journal for the Study of Time* 13, no.1: 7–27.
———. 2014. '"Err"menenutic of the "Word" and the "world": Categorizing/Interpreting Errors in James Joyce's *Ulysses*'. *The English and Foreign Languages Journal* 5, no.2: 59–79.
———. 2017a. *The Ontology of Gods: An Account of Enchantment, Disenchantment, and Re-enchantment*. New York: Palgrave Macmillan.
———. 2017b. '*Ce qui arrive (réellement)*: The Curious Relationship of the Word and the World, Against a Background of Discussing Deconstruction with Many Caveats'. In *Structure and Signs of Play: Derrida/Deconstruction@50*, edited by Pramod K. Nayar, 36–46. Mumbai: IRIS Knowledge Foundation.
Ghosh, Ranjan. 2012. 'Aesthetics of Hunger'. *Symploke* 19, no. 1–2: 143–57.

Ghosh, Ranjan, and J. Hillis Miller. 2016. *Thinking Literature across Continents*. Durham, NC: Duke University Press.
Gide, André. 1996. *The Immoralist*. Translated by Richard Howard. New York: Vintage.
Gilbert, Stuart. 1955. *James Joyce's* Ulysses: *A Study*. New York: Vintage.
Gottfried, Roy. 1995. *Joyce's Iritis and the Irritated Text: The Dis-Lexic Ulysses*. Gainesville, FL: University Press of Florida.
Grass, Günter. 1961. *The Tin Drum*. Translated by Ralph Manheim. New York: Penguin.
Green, Mitchell. 2010. 'How and What We Can Learn from Fiction'. In *A Companion to the Philosophy of Literature*, edited by Garry L. Hagberg and Walter Jost, 350–66. Malden, MA: Wiley-Blackwell.
Grésillon, Amuth. 2004. '**Still** *Lost Time*: **Already** the text of the *Recherche*'. In *Genetic Criticism: Texts and Avant-Textes*, edited by Jed Deppman, Daniel Ferrer and Michael Groden, 152–70. Philadelphia, PA: University of Pennsylvania Press.
Groden, Michael. 1977. Ulysses *in Progress*. Princeton, NJ: Princeton University Press.
Halliwell, Martin, and Andy Mousley. 2003. *Critical Humanisms: Humanist/Anti-Humanist Dialogues*. Edinburgh: Edinburgh University Press.
Hay, Louis. 1996. 'History or Genesis?' In *Drafts*, edited by Michel Contat, Denis Hollier and Jacques Neefs, translated by Ingrid Wassenaar, Special Issue of *Yale French Studies* 89: 191–207.
Heidegger, Martin. 1962. *Being and Time*. Translated by John Macquarrie and Edward Robinson. Oxford: Basil Blackwell.
Herman, Judith. 1997. *Trauma and Recovery: The Aftermath of Violence – From Domestic Abuse to Political Terror*. New York: Basic Books.
Horkheimer, Max, and Theodor W. Adorno. 2002. *Dialectic of Enlightenment: Philosophical Fragments*. Edited by Gunzelin Schmid Noerr, translated by Edmund Jephcott. Stanford, CA: Stanford University Press.
Hough, Graham. 1964. 'Crisis in Literary Education'. In *Crisis in the Humanities*, edited by J. H. Plumb, 96–109. Baltimore, MD: Penguin.
Huggan, Graham. 2001. *The Postcolonial Exotic: Marketing the Margins*. London: Routledge.
Jameson, Fredric. 1971. *Marxism and Form: Twentieth-Century Dialectical Theories of Literature*. Princeton, NJ: Princeton University Press.
Johnson, Samuel. 1765. 'Preface to Shakespeare'. Edited by Jack Lynch. Rutgers University. Accessed on 20 November 2012. http://andromeda.rutgers.edu/~jlynch/Texts/prefabr.html.
———. 1977. *Selected Poetry and Prose*. Edited by Frank Bady and W. K. Wimsatt. Berkeley, CA: University of California Press.
Jonson, Ben. 1910. 'To the Memory of my Beloved Master William Shakespeare, and What He Hath Left Us'. In *The Works of Ben Jonson*, vol. 3, 287–89. London: Chatto & Windus. Accessed on 20 August 2015. http://www.luminarium.org/sevenlit/jonson/benshake.htm.
Joyce, James. 1956. *Stephen Hero: Part of the First Draft of 'A Portrait of the Artist as a Young Man'*. Edited by Theodore Spencer. Rev. ed. London: Cape.
———. 1975. *Finnegans Wake*. London: Faber and Faber.
———. 1977. *A Portrait of the Artist as a Young Man: Text, Criticism, and Notes*. Edited by Chester G. Anderson. New York: Viking-Penguin.
———. 1984. *Ulysses: A Critical and Synoptic Edition*. 3 vols. Edited by Hans Walter Gabler, Wolfhard Steppe and Claus Melchior. New York: Garland.

Jung, Carl G. 1970. Carl Jung on *Ulysses*. In *James Joyce: The Critical Heritage*, edited by Robert H. Deming, 584–85. London: Routledge.

———. 1974. *Carl Jung: Letters*. Vol. 1. Translated by R. F. C. Hull, edited by Gerhard Adler and Aniela Jaffé. Princeton, NJ: Princeton University Press.

Kamuf, Peggy, ed. 1991. *A Derrida Reader: Between the Blinds*. New York: Columbia University Press.

Kant, Immanuel. 1997. 'Thoughts on Education'. In *Classic and Contemporary Readings in the Philosophy of Education*, edited by Steven M. Cahn. New York: McGraw Hill.

Keats, John. 1992. 'Letter to George and Thomas Keats'. In *Critical Theory since Plato*, edited by Hazard Adams. Rev. ed. Toronto: Thompson.

Kershner, Richard Brandon. 1996. *Joyce and Popular Culture*. Gainesville, FL: University Press of Florida.

Kiberd, Declan. 2009. *Ulysses and Us: The Art of Everyday Life in Joyce's Masterpiece*. New York: Norton.

Knapp, Stephen, and Walter Benn Michaels. 1982. 'Against Theory'. *Critical Inquiry* 8, no. 4: 723–42.

Kuhn, Thomas S. 1996. *The Structure of Scientific Revolutions*. 3rd ed. Chicago, IL: University of Chicago Press.

Kundera, Milan. 2004. *The Unbearable Lightness of Being*. Translated by Michael Henry Heim. New York: HarperCollins.

Leavis. F. R. 1936. *Revaluation: Tradition and Development in English Poetry*. London: Chatto and Windus.

Lejeune, Philippe. 2004. 'Auto-Genesis: Genetic Studies of Autobiographical Texts'. In *Genetic Criticism: Texts and Avant-Textes*, edited by Jed Deppman, Daniel Ferrer and Michael Groden, 193–217. Philadelphia, PA: University of Pennsylvania Press.

Levine, Jennifer. 2004. Ulysses. In *The Cambridge companion to James Joyce*, edited by Derek Attridge, 122–48. Cambridge: Cambridge University Press.

Lobsien, Eckhard. 1978. *Der Alltag des* Ulysses: *Die Vermittlung von ästhetischer und lebensweltlicher Erfahrung*. Stuttgart: Metzler.

Lowry, Elizabeth Schleber. 2017. *Invisible Hosts: Performing the Nineteenth-Century Spirit Medium's Autobiography*. Albany, NY: State University of New York Press.

Mackey, Peter Francis. 1999. *Chaos Theory and James Joyce's Everyman*. Gainesville, FL: University Press of Florida.

MacRae, Donald G. 1964. 'The Crisis of Sociology'. In *Crisis in the Humanities*, edited by J. H. Plumb, 124–38. Baltimore, MD: Penguin.

Maus, Katharine Eisaman. 1995. *Inwardness and Theater in the English Renaissance*. Chicago, IL: University of Chicago Press.

Miller, J. Hillis. 1976. 'Stevens' Rock and Criticism as Cure'. *Georgia Review* 30, no. 2: 330–48.

———. 1987. *The Ethics of Reading: Kant, de Man, Eliot, Trollope, James, and Benjamin*. New York: Columbia University Press.

———. 1991. *Theory Now and Then*. Hemel Hempstead: Harvester Wheatsheaf.

———. 1995. The Disputed Ground: Deconstruction and Literary Studies. In *Deconstruction Is/in America: A New Sense of the Political*, edited by Anselm Haverkamp, 79–86. New York: New York University Press.

Mill, John Stuart. 2012. 'Art as Intrinsic Personal Feeling'. In *Readings in the History of Aesthetics: An Open-Source Reader*. Accessed on 20 November 2012. http://philosophy.lander.edu/intro/artbook.html/x5988.htm.

Mitterand, Henri. 2004. 'Genetic Criticism and Cultural History: Zola's *Rougon-Macquart* dossiers'. In *Genetic Criticism: Texts and Avant-Textes*, edited by Jed Deppman, Daniel Ferrer and Michael Groden, 116–31. Philadelphia, PA: University of Pennsylvania Press.

Nabokov, Vladimir. 1982. *Lolita*. New York: Greenwich.

Nagel, Thomas. 1986. *The View from Nowhere*. Oxford: Oxford University Press.

Nietzsche, Friedrich. 1973. *The Portable Nietzsche*. Translated and edited by Walter Kaufmann. New York: Viking.

———. 2001. *The Gay Science*. Translated by Josefine Nauckhoff, edited by Bernard Williams. Cambridge: Cambridge University Press.

Nolan, Emer. 2007. 'James Joyce and the History of the Future'. In *Catholic Emancipations: Irish Fiction from Thomas Moore to James Joyce*, 150–80. Syracuse, NY: Syracuse University Press.

Norris, Christopher. 1988. 'Deconstruction, Post-Modernism and the Visual Arts'. In *What Is Deconstruction?*, edited by Christopher Norris and Andrew Benjamin, 7–33. London: Academy Editions/St Martin's Press.

Nussbaum, Martha C. 2001. 'The Transfiguration of Everyday Life: Joyce'. In *Upheavals of Thought: The Intelligence of Emotions*, 679–714. Cambridge: Cambridge University Press.

———. 2004. 'Finely Aware and Richly Responsible'. In *Philosophy of Literature: Contemporary and Classic Readings: An Anthology*, edited by Eileen John and Dominic McIver Lopes, 329–40. Malden, MA: Blackwell.

Olsen, Stein Haugom. 2010. 'Biography in Literary Criticism'. In *A Companion to the Philosophy of Literature*, edited by Garry L. Hagberg and Walter Jost, 436–52. Malden, MA: Wiley-Blackwell.

Ormiston, Gayle L., and Alan D. Schrift, ed. 1990. *The Hermeneutic Tradition: From Ast to Ricoeur*. Albany, NY: State University of New York Press.

Osteen, Mark. 1995. *The Economy of Ulysses: Making Both Ends Meet*. Syracuse, NY: Syracuse University Press.

Plumb, J. H., ed. 1964. *Crisis in the Humanities*. Baltimore, MD: Penguin.

Poirier, Richard. 1968. 'The Politics of Self-Parody'. *Partisan Review* 35, no. 3: 339–53.

Preece, Julian. 2009. 'Biography as Politics'. In *The Cambridge Companion to Günter Grass*, edited by Stuart Taberner, 10–23. Cambridge: Cambridge University Press.

Rabaté, Jean-Michel. 2001. *James Joyce and the Politics of Egoism*. Cambridge: Cambridge University Press.

Rabelais, François. 1936. *The Five Books of Gargantua and Pantagruel*. Translated by Jacques Le Clercq. New York: Modern Library-Random.

Radek, Karl. 1970. 'Karl Radek on Joyce's Realism'. In *James Joyce: The Critical Heritage*, edited by Robert H. Deming, 624–26. London: Routledge.

Rainey, Lawrence. 1999. 'The Cultural Economy of Modernism'. In *The Cambridge Companion to Modernism*, edited by Michael Levenson, 33–69. Cambridge: Cambridge University Press.

Ricoeur, Paul. 1981. *Hermeneutics and the Human Sciences: Essays on Language, Action and Interpretation*. Edited and translated by John B. Thompson. Cambridge: Cambridge University Press.

Robinson, Jenefer. 2010. 'Emotion and the Understanding of Narrative'. In *A Companion to the Philosophy of Literature*, edited by Garry L. Hagberg and Walter Jost, 71–92. Malden, MA: Wiley-Blackwell.

Rorty, Richard. 1982. *The Consequences of Pragmatism: Essays 1972–1980*. Minneapolis, MN: University of Minnesota Press.

———. 1990. *Philosophy and the Mirror of Nature*. London: Blackwell.

———. 1999. *Philosophy and Social Hope*. London: Penguin.
Russell, Bertrand. 1967. *A History of Western Philosophy*. New York: Simon and Schuster.
Said, Edward. 1994. *Culture and Imperialism*. London: Vintage.
Sargent, J.R. 1964. 'Economics: The Would-Be, May-Be Science'. In *Crisis in the Humanities*, edited by J. H. Plumb, 139–54. Baltimore, MD: Penguin.
Schlink, Bernhard. 1997. *The Reader*. Translated by Carol Brown Janeway. New York: Pantheon.
Schopenhauer, Arthur. 1968. *The World as Will and Representation*. Translated by E. F. J. Payne. Vol. 1. New York: Dover.
Schütze, Martin. 1962. *Academic Illusions in the Field of Letters and the Arts*. Hamden: Archon.
Scofield, C. I. 2006. Notes. *The Holy Bible Containing the Old and New Testaments: Reproduction of the First Scofield Reference Bible King James Version*. Sunbury, PA: Believers Bookshelf.
Scruton, Roger. 2010. 'Feeling Fictions'. In *A Companion to the Philosophy of literature*', edited by Garry L. Hagberg and Walter Jost, 93–105. Malden, MA: Wiley-Blackwell.
Shakespeare, William. 2011. *The Complete Works of William Shakespeare*. Project Gutenberg. Accessed on 29 June 2015. http://www.gutenberg.org/ebooks/100.
Shusterman, Richard. 2010. 'Literature and More than Literature'. In *A Companion to the Philosophy of Literature*, edited by Garry L. Hagberg and Walter Jost, 7–21. Malden, MA: Wiley-Blackwell.
Spengler, Oswald. 1926. *The Decline of the West*. 2 vols. Translated by Charles Francis Atkinson. New York: Knopf.
Spiegelman, Art. 1986. *Maus: A Survivor's Tale*. New York: Pantheon.
Spivak, Gayatri Chakravorty. 1974. 'Translator's Preface'. In *Of Grammatology* by Jacques Derrida, ix–lxxxix. Baltimore, MD: John Hopkins University Press.
———. 1988. 'Can the Subaltern Speak?' In *Marxism and the Interpretation of Culture*, edited by Cary Nelson and Lawrence Grossberg, 271–314. Urbana, IL: University of Illinois Press.
Stolnitz, Jerome. 2004. 'On the Cognitive Triviality of Art'. In *Philosophy of Literature: Contemporary and Classic Readings: An Anthology*, edited by Eileen John and Dominic McIver Lopes, 317–23. Malden, MA: Blackwell.
Stoppard, Tom. 1975. *Travesties*. New York: Grove Press.
Tarnas, Richard. 2010. *The Passion of the Western Mind: Understanding the Ideas That Have Shaped Our World View*. London: Pimlico.
Taylor, Charles. 1989. *Sources of the Self: The Making of the Modern Identity*. Cambridge: Cambridge University Press.
The Reader. 2008. Dir. Stephen Daldry. Germany: Mirage Enterprises and Neuente Babelsberg Film GmbH. Weinstein. Film.
Tolstoy, Leo. 1978. *Anna Karenina*. Moscow: Progress.
Troy. 2004. Dir. Wolfgang Peterson. USA: Warner Bros. Film.
Viollet, Catherine. 2004. 'Proust's "Confessions of a young girl": Truth or Fiction?'. In *Genetic Criticism: Texts and Avant-Textes*, edited by Jed Deppman, Daniel Ferrer and Michael Groden, 171–92. Philadelphia, PA: University of Pennsylvania Press.
Weber, Max. 2005. *Readings and Commentary on Modernity*. Edited by Stephen Kalberg. Malden, MA: Blackwell.
Wellhausen, Julius. 1957. *Prolegomena to the History of Ancient Israel*. Translated by J. Sutherland Black and Allan Menzies. New York: Meridian.
White, Hayden. 1973. *Metahistory: The Historical Imagination in Nineteenth-Century Europe*. Baltimore, MD: John Hopkins University Press.

Williams, Raymond. 1989. *Resources of Hope: Culture, Democracy, Socialism*. Edited by Robin Gable. London: Verso. Accessed on 15 September 2009. http://www.questia.com.

Wimsatt, William K, and Monroe C. Beardsley. 1946. 'The Intentional Fallacy'. *Sewanee Review* 54: 468–88.

Wittgenstein, Ludwig. 2001. *Philosophical Investigations: The German Text, with a Revised English Translation*. Translated by G. E. M. Anscombe. Oxford: Blackwell.

Wolfreys, Julian. 1998. *Deconstruction. Derrida*. New York: St Martin's Press.

Woodmansee, Martha, and Mark Osteen, ed. 1999. *The New Economic Criticism*. London: Routledge.

Woolf, Virginia. 1968. 'Modern Fiction'. *The Common Reader: First Series*. London: Hogarth Press, 184–95.

———. 1992. *The Waves*. Oxford: Oxford University Press.

———. [1929] 2004. *Jacob's Room*. London: Hogarth Press. ebooks@adelaide. University of Adelaide Library. Accessed on 5 September 2009. http://ebooks.adelaide.edu.au/w/woolf/virginia/w91j.

———. [1925] 2009. *Mrs Dalloway*. Oxford: Oxford University Press.

Wordsworth, William. 1800. *Preface to Lyrical Ballads*. Bartleby.com. Accessed on 20 November 2012. http://www.bartleby.com/39/36.html.

Molly Worthen. 2005. The Man on Whom Nothing was Lost: The Grand Strategy of Charles Hill. Boston, MA: Houghton Mifflin.

Zola, Émile. 1972. *Nana*. Translated by George Holden. London: Penguin.

INDEX

Abrams, M. H. 1, 46, 74, 94, 111
abstraction theory of knowledge vii, 20, 37
Abu Ghraib 23
Adorno, Theodor 99–100, 111, 114
Advaita (non-dualism) 39
aesthetic of frenzy 37
aesthetic of shock 46
Alltag 104, 115
Alltagsgeschichte 41
Althusser, Louis 26, 60, 111
analogous reasoning 3, 89–90, 102, 105
Anderson, Hans Christian 5
Annales School, the 27, 110
Antyodaya 63
Apophatic theology 65
Aristotle 19, 31–32, 50, 111
Arnold, Matthew 10, 96–97, 111
Auerbach, Erich 102, 111
Auschwitz 33, 45
auto-epiphany vii, 69–70
avant-garde 9, 30, 32, 40, 46–47, 99–100, 105, 109
avant-texte 76, 80, 85–88, 112–17

Barthes, Roland 7, 9, 50, 65, 74, 111
Baudelaire, Charles 13, 79
Beardsley, Monroe C. 26, 118
Bellini, Vincenzo 43
Benjamin, Walter 13, 115
Bentham, Jeremy 31
Bergson, Henri 19, 69
Bloch, Ernst 28, 111
Bloom, Harold 45, 53, 77, 94–95, 111
Braudel, Fernand 27, 103, 109–10, 112–13
Brecht, Bertolt 89, 112
bricoleur 60–61

Buddha, the 18
Burckhardt, Jacob 26
Butler, Judith 8

Camus, Albert 44
Carroll, Lewis 72–73
cathexis 37, 51, 58
chaos theory 57, 59, 90, 115
Cicero 6
civilization 15, 17, 27–28, 62, 112
classic viii, 3, 6, 96–97, 99–101, 106
cognitive ease, fallacy of 1, 12
cognitive miser theory 18, 59
Coleridge, Samuel Taylor 79
Comte, August 13
Conrad, Joseph 38
contestational reasoning 5
contrapuntal reading 58
counterculture 22
culture 1, 6, 12, 14–19, 22, 27, 29, 36, 40–41, 43, 45, 47, 49, 51, 62, 64, 69, 74, 77, 91, 93, 100, 109, 113, 115, 117–18
cultural casts 37
cultural fatalism 2, 60, 109
culture industry 100
curiosity for the singular 45

de Certeau, Michel 13
deconstruction vii, xi, 2–3, 53–54, 57, 65–71, 74, 86–87, 91, 97, 112–13, 115–16, 118
deductive reasoning vii, 2, 54, 86
defamiliarization 46
deism 25, 28
delicate epistemes vii, 2, 34, 39–41, 43, 47, 94–95, 104

Derrida, Jacques xi, 7, 49–50, 65–74, 77, 91, 111–13, 115, 117–18
de Saussure, Ferdinand 25–26, 91
Descartes, René 55
différance 66
de Man, Paul 71, 91, 112, 115
Dilthey, Wilhelm 8
discourse of qualification 3, 63
discourse of rights 3, 63
Disenchantment of the World 21, 25, 28, 78, 113
disponibilité 35
Dryden, John 44

Eagleton, Terry 9–10, 22, 25–26, 33–34, 61, 95, 97, 113
Educational Perennialism 12
Einstein, Albert 8, 70
Eliade, Mircea 44, 113
Eliot, T. S. 10, 32, 80, 101, 113, 115
epiphany/epiphanies vii, 37–38, 40, 69–70, 102, 104, 111
episteme vii, 2, 34, 39–41, 43, 47, 50, 70, 94–95, 104, 106
epistemic violence 56
Erikson, Erik 109
Erklären 8
existentialism 50
extrinsic criticism 55

feminism 53, 64, 70–71, 87, 93, 95, 107
Final Solution, the 23
Fish, Stanley 47, 113
Fiske, Susan T. 18, 59, 113
flâneur 13
Flaubert, Gustave 80–81, 113
Formalism 25, 46
Foucault, Michel 50, 60, 64, 68, 106, 113
Frank, Anne 87–88
Frankl, Viktor 23, 113
Freud, Sigmund 23, 46, 51, 58, 73, 98, 109, 113

Gabler, Hans Walter 51, 76, 114
Gasché, Rodolphe 70–71, 91, 113
Geisteswissenschaften 8
Gelegenheitsdenken 15
genetic criticism 3, 75–76, 78–88, 91, 105, 112–17

Genette, Gérard 76, 113
Ghosh, Ranjan 51, 113–14
Gide, André 36, 51, 114
God-signifier 49
Goethe, Johann Wolfgang von 14–15, 17, 33, 39, 79
Götterdämmerung 28
Grass, Günter 41–43, 51, 97–98, 114, 116

Hegel, Georg Wilhelm Friedrich 15, 18–19, 59, 69, 109
Heidegger, Martin 7, 11, 55, 68, 70, 114
Heisenberg, Werner 8, 70
hermeneutic of epistemic fastidiousness 2, 39
hermeneutic of possibilities 58, 109
hermeneutics of faith 58
heremeneutics of suspicion 57–58, 109
Herman, Judith 23, 114
histoire conjoncturale 27
histoire des mentalités 22
histoire événementielle 27
histoire structurale 27
historical a priori 106
Hochkulturen 15
Holocaust, the 7, 39
Homer 6, 62, 78, 83–84, 91, 98–99
horizon of expectations 47
Huggan, Graham 45, 114
humanism/humanist vii, 1–2, 8, 20, 25, 30–31, 54, 61–64, 66, 90, 112, 114
humanities vii, 1, 5–9, 11, 13, 20, 22, 25–26, 56, 86, 114–17
human world process vii, 1, 5, 12–14, 20–22, 25–26, 37

ideological criticism vii, 2, 5, 9, 26, 33, 53–54, 57–61, 68, 97
ideology 2–3, 13, 22, 26, 29, 33, 54, 57–61, 68–69, 74, 85, 87, 91, 93, 106, 108–9, 111, 113
Ideological State Apparatuses 60, 111
implementational intelligence 1, 11
interpellation 60
interpretive strategies 47
intrinsic criticism 55, 57
Irigaray, Luce 64
Iterability 49–50, 67, 97

James, Henry 35, 46
Jameson, Fredric 89, 102, 114
James, William 40
Jauss, Hans Robert 47
jeu 66, 69
Johnson, Samuel 32, 78
Jolas, Eugene 46, 99
Jonson, Ben 96, 114
Joyce, James x, 38, 43–44, 46, 53, 57, 71–73, 76, 80, 82–84, 88–89, 91, 98–106, 109–16
Jung, Carl Gustav 23–24, 73, 99, 115

Kant, Immanuel 7, 10–11, 16, 19, 56, 69, 90, 115
katabasis 85
Keats, John 35, 115
Knights, L. C. 10
Kuhn, Thomas 70, 106, 115
Kundera, Milan 37, 46, 115

language-game 31
Leavis, F. R. 32, 115
Lebenswelt 21, 48, 69, 89, 115
Lévi-Strauss, Claude 26
Lewis, C. S. 85
linguistic turn 68
literature as hunger 51
logocentrism 67
Logos 19, 67
Logotherapy 23, 113
longue durée 27
Lyotard, Jean-François 9

macro-concepts 2, 30–31, 66
Mallarmé, Stéphane 38
Mann, Thomas 15
Marxism 26, 50, 53, 59, 89, 102, 114, 117
Marxist criticism 26, 33, 53, 59, 70, 87, 93, 95, 102, 114, 117
Marx, Karl 58
masters of suspicion 58, 70
matrix of dialectical correspondences 49
Mayakovsky, Vladimir 51
medieval 14, 21, 50, 85
metacognition 60
micro-concepts 2, 30–31, 66
middle ages 21
milestone approach viii, 3, 101

Miller, Arthur 6
Miller, J. Hillis 70–71, 73, 114–15
Mill, John Stuart 32–33
mimemata/mimesis 31–32, 111
mimetic 33, 46, 73, 84
minimalist criterion of knowledge 1, 9
modernism/modernist 14, 30, 32–33, 40, 44, 46–48, 72, 80, 84, 89, 91, 99–101, 109, 112, 116
Morrison, Toni 24

Nabokov, Vladimir 38–39, 44, 88, 116
nacheinander 72, 84, 91
Nagel, Thomas 55, 116
Naturwissenschaften 8
nebeneinander 72, 84, 91
negative capability 35
New Criticism 40, 86
New Historicism 30, 76, 95, 107
Nietzsche, Friedrich 15, 42, 48, 58, 61, 64, 68–69, 91, 112, 116
Nussbaum, Martha 32, 102, 116

ontology of the intangible vii, 1, 22, 26, 39
orature 107

paradigm shift 23, 61, 70, 82, 106
Paris, Jean 101, 109
penchant for embeddedness 2, 58
philosophemes 66
phronesis 50
Plumb, J. H. 6, 114–17
Poe, Edgar Allan 39, 79
Poiesis 31, 109
Polis 16, 19
popular culture 100, 109, 115
postcolonialism 9, 45, 53, 62, 64, 70, 93–95, 107, 114
postmodernism 8–9, 32
post-structuralism ix, 2, 9, 26, 30, 66, 74, 78–79, 86, 112
Pound, Ezra 46, 91
praxis 24, 31, 103
Presocratics 19
process metaphysics 10
Proust, Marcel 33, 80–82, 117
psychoanalysis 73, 109
psychoanalytic criticism 70, 87
Pushkin, Alexander 25

Radek, Karl 102, 116
Ragnarök 28
Ranke, Leopold von 12
reader-text symmetry vii, 2, 10, 39, 47–48
reflective intelligence vii, 1, 11
Renaissance, the 22, 26, 36, 90–91, 115
Repressive State Apparatuses 60
Richter, Johann Paul Friedrich 2, 45
Ricoeur, Paul 57–58, 70, 116
Rimbaud, Arthur 38
Romanticism 17, 32, 40, 79, 81
Rorty, Richard 5–6, 61, 116
Roy, Arundhati 47
Rushdie, Salman 76
Ruskin, John 63

Said, Edward 58, 117
Sargent, J. R. 10, 117
Sartre, Jean-Paul 80, 85
Schiller, Friedrich 28
Schlegel, Friedrich 79
Schlink, Bernhard 32, 34, 117
School of Resentment 53, 77, 94–95
Schopenhauer, Arthur 18–19, 69, 117
scientistic aspirations vii, 1, 25, 86
Seeck, Otto 17
Seneca 29
sensation hunger 37, 45
Shakespeare, William 10, 32, 36, 41, 72, 76, 83, 87, 94–96, 98, 108, 114, 117
singularity 45–46
Spengler, Oswald 14–19, 26–28, 69, 117
Spiegelman, Art 39, 117
Spivak, Gayatri Chakravorty 56, 64, 73, 117
Stein, Gertrude 46
Stoppard, Tom 110, 117
Stowe, Harriet Beecher 32
Strachey, James 51
strategic essentialism 64
Structuralism 26, 79, 86, 112
Structural Marxism 26
Swift, Jonathan 44
symmetric ontology 50
sympathetic empiricism 39

Tarnas, Richard 19–20, 117
Taylor, Charles 102, 117
Taylor, Shelley E. 18, 59, 113
technê 50
templates of significance vii, 2, 34, 43–44
temporal ontology viii, 3, 77
textualism of faith 50
theoria 31
Tolstoy, Leo 45, 117
Tzara, Tristan 110

Übermensch 42
unheimlich 45
Untermensch 42, 63
Utilitarianism 15

Verfremdung 89
Versluis, Arthur 39
Verstehen 8
versus fixation 109
Vorstruktur 55

Weber, Max 25, 28, 117
Weltanschauung 15, 89
Weltschmerzen 2, 44
White, Hayden 12, 88, 117
Whitehead, A. N. 10
Wiesel, Elie 24
Wilde, Oscar 33
Williams, Raymond 76, 109, 118
will to meaning 24
will to reality 12
Wimsatt, William K. 26, 114, 118
Wittgenstein, Ludwig 31, 66
Woolf, Virginia 35, 38, 105, 118
Wordsworth, William 32–33, 39, 79, 118
world-appetite vii, 2, 23, 34, 44–45, 47, 51
world-conceptualization 3, 69
world-excess 3, 70
World War I 35
World War II 15, 17, 22, 27, 32, 48

Yeats, William Butler 45, 80, 99

Zeitgeist 12, 102
Zola, Émile 46, 80, 87, 116, 118

www.ingramcontent.com/pod-product-compliance
Lightning Source LLC
Chambersburg PA
CBHW021833300426
44114CB00009BA/428